THE GROWING CRISIS OF AFRICA'S ORPHANS

HEARING

BEFORE THE

SUBCOMMITTEE ON AFRICA, GLOBAL HEALTH,
GLOBAL HUMAN RIGHTS, AND INTERNATIONAL
ORGANIZATIONS

OF THE

COMMITTEE ON FOREIGN AFFAIRS
HOUSE OF REPRESENTATIVES

ONE HUNDRED THIRTEENTH CONGRESS

SECOND SESSION

JULY 16, 2014

Serial No. 113–198

Printed for the use of the Committee on Foreign Affairs

Available via the World Wide Web: http://www.foreignaffairs.house.gov/ or
http://www.gpo.gov/fdsys/

U.S. GOVERNMENT PRINTING OFFICE

88–733PDF   WASHINGTON : 2014

For sale by the Superintendent of Documents, U.S. Government Printing Office
Internet: bookstore.gpo.gov   Phone: toll free (866) 512–1800; DC area (202) 512–1800
Fax: (202) 512–2104   Mail: Stop IDCC, Washington, DC 20402–0001

CONTENTS

THE GROWING CRISIS OF AFRICA'S ORPHANS

WEDNESDAY, JULY 16, 2014

House of Representatives,
Subcommittee on Africa, Global Health,
Global Human Rights, and International Organizations,
Committee on Foreign Affairs,
Washington, DC.

The subcommittee met, pursuant to notice, at 2:01 p.m., in room 2172, Rayburn House Office Building, Hon. Christopher H. Smith (chairman of the subcommittee) presiding.

Mr. SMITH. The subcommittee will come to order.

Good afternoon, everyone.

Today's hearing addresses a very important humanitarian crisis: The more than 50 million children orphaned on the continent of Africa. Indeed, to put this in perspective, as one of our witnesses today, Shimwaayi Muntemba, has pointed out, with such a number, the orphans of Africa, if grouped together in a single country, would be the fourth-largest country in all of Africa after Nigeria, Ethiopia, and the Democratic Republic of the Congo.

The factors contributing to this crisis are varied, starting with civil war and civil unrest, which have displaced millions, wars that have led to the deaths of parents and other adult relatives, leaving children to fend for themselves, or sometimes children who are separated from their parents in a mad flight for sanctuary, never learning if their moms or dads are alive or dead. They may never know if they are orphaned in reality or if both parents turn out to have survived and are alive in a refugee camp somewhere else. Such parents, too, agonize over what ever happened to their beloved children.

Other children are indirect victims of the HIV/AIDS pandemic, which has wreaked such devastating havoc on the continent, or other diseases. They could have lost one or both parents to this or some other dreaded disease.

Often being forced into the role of primary caretaker of younger siblings, their childhood innocence is ended by the burdens of adult responsibility.

As with many of the humanitarian crises that confront the continent, there is a big-picture aspect to this one and one which we as Congress certainly need to address. There are important strategic implications of so many children and adolescents left without moms or dads.

We have all heard of the scourge of child soldiers, how orphaned children are recruited and brutalized, themselves, into becoming

(1)

remorseless killers. Terrorist groups, such as the Lord's Resistance Army under the rapacious warlord Joseph Kony, actively recruit child soldiers. Perhaps our State Department witness, the Honorable Robert Jackson, with his vast depth of regional knowledge, may address that in his remarks today.

And if humanitarian reasons are not enough to compel Congress to rally behind the efforts to address the issue of Africa's orphans by USAID and countless other charitable organizations, many of them faith-based, then strategic concerns and the effect that this has on the stability throughout the region should be a reason to sit up and take notice of this tragedy.

But behind every statistic about an orphaned child or children, behind the pie charts and graphs, there is also a portrait in miniature: A lonely child who is left without a mother or a father, perhaps dealing each night with the pangs of hunger or just seeking a place where he or she can lay down his or her head in safety until the morning comes. That child awakes to forage and to fend for another day.

Behind every statistic, there is a young boy or girl who has to deal with the sense of abandonment or with the trauma of having seen parents killed before his or her own eyes; there is a little soul, a young person, whose inherent dignity has been scarred in a world itself wounded, where there is so much pain, suffering, and darkness.

These children are in need of love and compassion, of simple needs being met. Those who find loving homes and families are truly the lucky ones. One remedy for this crisis is inter-country adoption, which sometimes brings children from Africa to our shores to provide them with loving homes.

This is, of course, only a partial remedy, because for every child who is given a loving home, there are many more for whom there will never be such a refuge. At best, they may end up in an institutional orphanage, which is a topic fraught with controversy. While the best ones—again, often faith-based—help address the developmental and education needs of children, the worst may abet human trafficking.

In some cases, such institutions do not even shelter orphans per se, but, rather, children are placed there by parents who think that their children will get a better education and nutrition than what they themselves can provide. Clearly, such institutions can never provide the type of love that a father and a mother, along with any siblings, can provide.

One issue that will be addressed in our second panel today, then, is the role of inter-country adoption in helping address, at least in part, the crisis of orphans. Some of the testimony will be critical of the role of our State Department's Office of Children's Issues in the Bureau of Consular Affairs. Such testimony needs to be heard, for we can and we must, all of us, do better.

We will also hear about an adoption issue that has received a lot of attention on Capitol Hill and was the topic of a resolution authored by my good friend and colleague, Collin Peterson of Minnesota, which I am happy to say was passed by the House of Representatives just a few weeks ago after being marked up by our subcommittee and then the full Foreign Affairs Committee.

Last year, the DRC suspended the issuance of exit permits for Congolese children adopted by foreign parents, impacting hundreds of U.S. families. The suspension means that the Congolese children adopted by American parents simply cannot leave the country to go to their new homes even though the parents have been officially declared the legal guardians under Congolese law.

What's more, despite the exit-permit suspension, Congolese courts have continued processing new adoptions, leading to a backlog of adopted children who are unable to leave the country. More than 800 American families are caught up, in varying degrees, of this adoption limbo, breaking hearts.

This is a deplorable situation for these children and for their distraught families, as well. Indeed, we will hear about this from one such family that has been impacted, as well as an advocate for families that in like manner have been impacted.

Finally, I also want to say a word to those parents here today who have endured not only burdens that are financial but ones that are primarily emotional, separated from the children they have voluntarily and lovingly welcomed into their lives.

Your hardship and pain is deeply noted by my colleagues and I, as well as our staff members, many of whom have worked not only on passing Congressman Peterson's resolution but have also promoted within our State Department and the Government of the DRC some effective and durable remedies to these situations. Please continue to persevere. Don't give up hope. Both the executive branch and the legislative branch are firmly in your corner.

I would like to new yield to Karen Bass, the ranking member.

Ms. BASS. Thank you, Mr. Chair, as always, for your leadership on this and so many other issues.

I would also like to thank our distinguished witnesses, including the Honorable Robert Jackson, Principal Deputy Assistant Secretary in the Bureau of African Affairs; the Honorable Nancy Lindborg, Assistant Administrator in the Bureau for Democracy, Conflict and Humanitarian Assistance; and humanitarian and advocacy experts from the civil society.

According to UNICEF, in 2012 there were an estimated 56 million orphaned children in Africa, of whom an estimated 27 percent were orphaned due to HIV/AIDS.

Numerous sources suggest orphans typically consist of a number of our most vulnerable children, who have been or could become victims of trafficking, child labor, violence, and abuse. We can't allow children under any circumstances to be subject to such brutality. Congress should do all we can to ensure that all children can grow up in loving and caring homes.

I am a proud cosponsor of Children in Families First, which is led by my esteemed colleague, Senator Landrieu. This legislation can be one of the solutions to addressing the issue of orphaned children, not only in Africa but around the world.

CHIFF, as we are calling it, Children in Families First, which aims to redirect some U.S. resources to focus more on ensuring that all children grow up in families, draws on the strength of agencies to achieve that goal.

As we prepare to hear from today's witnesses, I hope we can learn lessons from their expertise and use their knowledge to improve conditions for orphaned children in Africa. I am committed to working toward this end and look forward to working with my colleagues to find the most effective and sustainable solutions.

Mr. SMITH. Thank you very much.

Because of time limitations, would you like to give a brief opening statement?

Mr. BERA. Yeah, just very quickly, I want to thank the chairman and ranking member for, obviously, a very important hearing. We still have a long ways to go, though, I would say. Thank you.

Mr. SMITH. Thank you, Dr. Bera.

As John Lennon said in "The Ballad of John and Yoko Ono," it's good to have the both of you back.

We have two very distinguished government leaders providing testimony.

But, very briefly, Nancy Lindborg is the Assistant Administrator for the Bureau of Democracy, Conflict and Humanitarian Assistance at USAID. She has testified before our subcommittee on numerous occasions.

Since assuming her office in 2010, Ms. Lindborg has led DCHA teams in response to the ongoing Syria crisis, the Horn of Africa in 2011, Sahel in 2012 droughts, the Arab Spring, the aftermath of Typhoon Haiyan in the Philippines, and numerous other global crises.

Prior to joining USAID, she was president of Mercy Corps, where she spent 14 years doing that wonderful work of protecting the weak and the vulnerable.

We will also then hear from Ambassador Robert Jackson, who is currently Principal Deputy Assistant Secretary to Bureau of African Affairs.

He previously served as Ambassador to Cameroon as well as Deputy Chief of Mission and Charge at the U.S. Embassies in Morocco and Senegal. He has also served at U.S. Embassies in Burundi, Zimbabwe, Portugal, and Canada.

At the State Department headquarters, he has worked in commercial and consular sections and conducted officer training. He has also performed oversight work in the Office for the Promotion of Democracy and Human Rights after 9/11.

Ambassador Jackson has appeared before this subcommittee, again, on many, many occasions. And welcome back.

Ms. Lindborg, please go first.

STATEMENT OF THE HONORABLE NANCY LINDBORG, ASSISTANT ADMINISTRATOR, BUREAU FOR DEMOCRACY, CONFLICT AND HUMANITARIAN ASSISTANCE, U.S. AGENCY FOR INTERNATIONAL DEVELOPMENT

Ms. LINDBORG. Chairman Smith, Ranking Member Bass, members of the subcommittee, thank you very much for inviting me to testify today.

And, Chairman Smith, I want to specifically acknowledge your extraordinary leadership on human rights and humanitarian assistance worldwide. So, many thanks.

Africa, as we know, is a continent on the rise. It has growing economies and the youngest population in the world. Fifty percent of the population of sub-Saharan Africa is under the age of 18. So there is an extraordinary potential for this generation of youth to shape the future in powerful ways.

However, more than 200 million of these children currently live in extreme poverty, over 15 million children have lost one or more parents to AIDS, and millions more, as we have heard, are affected by conflict and natural disaster.

I have personally seen what happens to the children and families who are affected by these conflicts. Often, the shocks are coming one after another. And we also have seen the enormous difference that USAID-supported programs can make in the lives of these affected.

I want to just cite Nyawal Ruach, a 29-year-old mother in Bor, Sudan. And, during the recent violence, she saw conflict coming toward her house. She tied her two young sons together so she wouldn't lose them, but they nonetheless got swept away in the crowds. And it was through a U.S.-supported center that reunited families that she was able to find her sons again. In the middle of a conflict, that is a powerful and important thing to have happen.

The United States has long been the largest donor for orphans and vulnerable children. And, in 2005, a very important law, Public Law 109–95, passed and that, coupled with the learnings from an evidence summit in 2011, really helped us to galvanize across the entire interagency and prompt us to create an Action Plan on Children in Adversity. And so, for the first time, we now have across the interagency a common framework and a shared language that really pulls together the efforts of seven agencies across the U.S. Government.

And, as you noted, Chairman Smith, there are many causes of adversity, from conflict to poverty to HIV/AIDS, but this framework helps us understand and stay focused on the three overarching, interrelated objectives that we know are the most important for making a difference in the life of a child. So I want to just quickly talk about those three objectives.

The first is, Africa has seen extraordinary progress in reducing the number of children who die before their fifth birthday. These mortality rates have been reduced by almost half in 20 years. We stand within reach of ending preventable child and maternal deaths by 2035. That is extraordinary.

We also know that keeping children alive is also just the first step. We know that the first 1,000 days between a woman's pregnancy and a child's second birthday lays the foundation for your entire life, for your lifelong health and your future development.

So the first objective of our action plan is to build strong beginnings. And we are helping to build the long-term health of children through nutrition, through health. We have a new USAID nutrition policy, and our Office of Food for Peace is applying the best of nutritional science to reformulate special foods that meet the nutritional needs of children under 2 with more therapeutic food products.

We have also seen increasing evidence of the essential need for nurture and emotional support during these early, critical formative years. And studies have shown that excessive stress can actually have the same effect on a developing brain as malnutrition.

A very powerful story that has informed this was that, following the genocide in Rwanda, when 1 million refugees poured into what was then Zaire, in an effort to save lives, infants and children were separated from their families and essentially laid out on beds so they could receive vaccines and IV nutritional feeding, yet they still died by the hundreds. And what we learned from that was the phenomenon called ''failure to thrive,'' that they lacked the human contact and nurture that is required to grow and to develop.

This was a very painful and powerful lesson, but that has led to our second objective of the action plan, which is called ''Put Families First.''

Evidence has shown that families, extended families, including parents, grandparents, relatives, foster or adoptive families, are the best source of support for children. Yet we know that about 46 million children in Africa have lost one parent and over 10 million have lost both.

The vast majority outside of family care do have parents and relatives, and there is a rich tradition of kinship care in Africa. So getting children into families and strengthening the ability of those families to care and protect is a significant critical priority in both our humanitarian and development programming.

And to do so, our programs support families struggling to provide care for vulnerable children by connecting them with a range of help options, whether it is urgent material needs, financial needs, long-term family income generation, or access to health and treatment services. We aim to empower them to decide what is best for their families so they can care for their children.

The third objective of the Action Plan on Children in Adversity is to protect children, particularly at an early age. Across the continent, we are targeting vulnerable children, including, as you have noted, child soldiers, street children, children accused of witchcraft, children lost in the legal system, children with disabilities, child laborers, and HIV/AIDS orphans.

A goal is to support children's reintegration into communities to help children and youth get the kind of life and vocational skills that can set them on a pathway, strengthen local groups in their ability to contribute to advocating for children's rights in their communities.

We focus on providing safe spaces for children to heal, to learn; give parents and other caregivers time to address their own needs and those of their families. So this includes outreach, direct support for parents, and really tries to decrease the risk of family separation or child labor.

Very importantly, we also focus on strengthening country systems. This is a key component of success, as we help local and national governments take a critical, more active role in supporting their own children.

We know that if we don't focus on the child we lose the person. And we know that investments in a strong start for Africa's children are absolutely critical to lay a foundation for a healthy, productive future for Africa itself. So USAID remains very committed to meeting the needs of vulnerable children in Africa, while also reducing the root issues that create those conditions for conflict and abuse.

We very much look forward to continuing the cooperation of the work across the U.S. Government, and especially with this subcommittee, in our shared commitment to promote healthy, resilient families and communities where children can thrive.

Thank you.

Mr. SMITH. Ms. Lindborg, thank you very much for your testimony.

[The prepared statement of Ms. Lindborg follows:]

Nancy E. Lindborg
Assistant Administrator for Democracy, Conflict and Humanitarian Assistance
U.S. Agency for International Development

House Foreign Affairs Committee
Subcommittee on Africa, Global Health, Global Human Rights, and International
Organizations
July 16, 2014

"The Growing Crisis of Africa's Orphans"

Chairman Smith, Ranking Member Bass and Members of the Subcommittee, thank you for
inviting me to testify on USAID's response to orphaned and vulnerable children in Africa. Thank
you also for your support for USAID's humanitarian and development programs around the
globe.

Introduction

Africa is a continent on the rise, with growing economies and the youngest population in the
world. With fifty percent of the population in Sub-Saharan Africa under the age of 18, there is
extraordinary potential for this generation of youth to shape the future of the continent in
powerful ways. However, more than 200 million of these children currently live in extreme
poverty, over 15 million children have lost one or both parents to AIDS, and millions more are
affected by conflict and natural disaster.

I've personally seen what happens to children in families facing one catastrophe after another,
often unable to buffer the compounding shocks. In March of this year, I visited South Sudan,
where violence and insecurity have forced more than one and a half million people from their
homes since mid-December. Among those fleeing are thousands of children separated from their
families – some sent to safety by parents desperate to save their children. Others became
separated from their parents during the recent violence that has ravaged their country.

While the needs and challenges in these settings are often overwhelming, I have seen the
enormous difference USAID-supported programs can make in the lives of those affected.
Nyawal Ruach, a 29-year old mother from Bor in South Sudan, is one of the people we've
helped. As she heard the fighting approach, she tied her two boys together to ensure they would
not get lost from each other. Despite her efforts, the boys were swept up in the chaos and
separated from her as they followed others running to escape the violence. It was at a USAID-
supported center established to trace families and rescue lost children where Ms. Ruach found
her two sons.

Our efforts, not only in Africa but around the world, are supporting and enabling mothers like
Nyawal and many other parents to care for their children. This type of support is aimed at
preventing unnecessary family-child separation, promoting appropriate, protective and
permanent family care, and ensuring that children not only survive but also thrive. And as we
meet the needs of vulnerable children, USAID, as embodied in our new mission statement,

focuses also on the underlying drivers that create these crises, partnering to end extreme poverty and promote resilient, democratic societies.

To talk about children in adversity in Africa is to open a very broad conversation that encompasses issues ranging from access to education to lack of economic opportunity. However, for the purposes of this hearing, I would like focus on three main objectives in line with the U.S. Government Action Plan on Children in Adversity to help vulnerable children in Africa and around the world. These three objectives include supporting strong, healthy beginnings; strengthening families and communities so they can protect and promote the well-being and development of children; and the prevention, response, and protection of children from violence, exploitation, abuse, and neglect.

The U.S. Government Action Plan and USAID's Programmatic Response

For over twenty years, USAID has led efforts to focus on children in adversity through the Agency's programming worldwide, including our Displaced Children and Orphans Fund. USAID is the lead agency under 2005 Public Law 109-95: *The Assistance for Orphans and Other Vulnerable Children in Developing Countries Act*, and we house the U.S. Government Special Advisor on Children in Adversity and the Center on Children in Adversity. The Advisor and Center both work to strengthen the efforts of the seven U.S. federal agencies working on the behalf of children and oversee the coordination and implementation of the Action Plan on Children in Adversity.

The Action Plan is a whole-of-government strategy for helping children. Its goal is to ensure that more children grow up within protective family care, free from deprivation, exploitation, and danger. Launched from the White House in December 2012, the Action Plan is grounded in evidence that shows a promising future belongs to those nations that invest wisely in their children, while failure to do so undermines social and economic progress. The Action Plan focuses and coordinates programs throughout the U.S. Government to achieve our three primary objectives: build strong beginnings, put family care first, and protect children.

Across these objectives we face the struggle of determining an accurate accounting for how many children are separated from their families. In response, USAID is developing innovative tools and partnerships that can help us better understand, account for, and track the numbers of children outside of family care, especially in situations of crisis and conflict. Working with Save the Children, for example, we are developing methods to estimate the number of children living outside of family care in disaster settings and testing them on the ground in North Kivu, Democratic Republic of Congo (DRC). Separately, in collaboration with Columbia University, we are working to identify children outside of family care and develop a scorecard that governments and organizations can use to measure their success in reducing the numbers of children outside of families across a broad set of development contexts.

Building Strong Beginnings

Under the first objective, *building strong beginnings*, we have achieved remarkable results in combating preventable child death and helping all children reach their fifth birthday. And we know the challenge is not only to help children survive but also thrive. USAID does this through comprehensive programs that promote sound development of children by integrating health, nutrition, and family support.

Africa has seen significant progress in reducing under-five mortality rates from 180 deaths per 1,000 live births in 1990 to 98 in 2012. As a result of sustained global commitment and growing country ownership, we stand within reach of achieving a goal critical to addressing the crisis of orphans in Africa – a goal once unimaginable: ending preventable child and maternal deaths by 2035. To target the more than 6.6 million children globally under-five who will die this year of largely preventable causes, USAID has narrowed our focus on child and maternal health to the 24 countries - including 17 in Sub-Saharan Africa - that represent more than 70 percent of maternal and child deaths in the developing world.

Evidence has affirmed that the first 1,000 days between a woman's pregnancy and her child's second birthday lays the foundation for a person's lifelong health and future development. To ensure healthier children and more productive communities in the poorest regions of the world, USAID's Office of Food for Peace is applying the best of nutrition science to better target the special nutritional needs of vulnerable groups, particularly women and children under two. USAID now uses ready-to-use therapeutic and supplementary foods designed to treat and prevent malnutrition, as well as better fortified commodities. USAID has set a goal to meet 10 percent of UNICEF's global requirement for ready-to-use therapeutic food and 10 percent of the World Food Program's global requirement for ready-to-use supplementary food to help tackle this burgeoning problem in crisis zones such as South Sudan and Central African Republic.

Additionally, the U.S. Government's Global Health Initiative, Feed the Future, and the U.S. President's Emergency Plan for AIDS Relief have comprehensive strategies in health and nutrition to reach chronically underserved children in their early years.

For example, USAID is working with CARE International to implement a multi-faceted program targeting working mothers with young children in rural Kamonyi District, southern Rwanda. The diverse services offered are designed to support families in a variety of ways over the course of several years. The program includes home-based daycare, community-based child development centers for preschoolers, parenting education on child development topics, children's rights, and income-generating activities. The daycare and preschool centers not only provide meals for the attendees, but also serve as venues for community health workers to conduct monthly check-ups that ensure children who become ill or whose growth falters are quickly identified for treatment.

Strengthening Families and Caregivers

The second objective of the Action Plan is to *put family care first*. Evidence clearly shows that families – parents, grandparents, relatives, foster families or adoptive families – are the best source of support for children. A National Institutes of Health-funded study of children in institutions in Romania, for example, showed significant deficits in IQ for children in institutions versus those in families. The study also showed that when these children were placed with families at a young age, their IQ nearly rebounded to that of their peers; however, when left in institutions, there was little or no gain.

Yet we know that there are about 56 million children in Africa who have lost one or both parents - of which over 10 million have lost both parents. Our assistance supports and enables families to provide basic care for their children, prevents unnecessary family-child separation, and promotes appropriate, protective and permanent family care.

In Africa, the vast majority of children outside of family care do have parents or relatives, and there is a rich tradition of kinship care in Africa. Therefore, getting children into families and strengthening their ability to care and protect is a top priority.

Family unification or reunification and supporting families struggling to provide care for vulnerable children includes strategies such as deinstitutionalizing separated children; increasing family income generation; providing conditional cash transfers; meeting urgent material needs such as food, clothing, and shelter; linking families to appropriate treatment or services; and ensuring parents and caregivers have the knowledge and skills needed to decide what is best for themselves and their families.

In Liberia, for example, approximately 5,000 children live in 114 orphanages, though 88 percent of these children have at least one living parent. Over the past two years, our program partner has placed more than 1,100 children in family care, including more than 500 children previously living in orphanages, and more than 600 who had been living on the street. At the same time, the program supports education and health care, and builds the capacity of local government social services so they can continue this work.

On the other side of the continent in Ethiopia, at least 7,000 children live in orphanages. With support from USAID, the Ethiopian Ministry of Justice conducted a study of more than 100 residential institutions, resulting in the government's immediate declaration to close 45 substandard institutions. In the last two years, close to 1,000 children have been moved from these inadequate institutions and placed in family care.

Also in Ethiopia, the PEPFAR-supported *Yekokeb Birhan*, the second largest Orphans and Vulnerable Children program in Africa, has supported 76,000 households caring for orphans and vulnerable children through economic strengthening activities. Seventy-five percent of those households now have regular income and improved access to education, health and other critical services. School attendance has increased by 14 percent, with a 71 percent increase in the number of children enrolled in pre-school programs. Full immunization rates jumped from 34 percent at the start of the program to 58 percent - higher than the national average.

We also work to put appropriate family care first through our humanitarian programming. The U.S. Government, through USAID and the U.S. Department of State's Bureau of Population, Refugees, and Migration, is the single largest contributor to programs focused on addressing the safety and well-being of children in humanitarian situations around the world. In FY2013 alone, USAID allocated more than $17 million in funding to support programs aimed at building knowledge, tools, and capacity to address child protection in 15 conflict and disaster-affected countries - 11 of which are in Africa.

Since the onset of violence in South Sudan on December 15, USAID has helped launch five programs dedicated to identifying and supporting boys and girls who have become separated from their families and reuniting them with surviving caregivers, when possible. Working with UNICEF and other partners, we have identified more than 3,000 unaccompanied, separated, and missing boys and girls–and reunited more than 400 with their families.

In an effort to improve and streamline the reunification process, we have invested in UNICEF's Rapid Family Tracing and Reunification tool - an open source application for handheld devices that assists child protection workers in the field. With this application, humanitarian workers can use cellphones and other mobile devices to input data and quickly share information with other child protection workers throughout the affected country and across borders. As a result, the length of time children are separated from families and vulnerable to exploitation, violence, and abuse is greatly diminished.

Child Protection

The third objective of the Action Plan on Children in Adversity is to *protect children*. Global studies show that about 36 percent of girls and 29 percent of boys worldwide have been sexually abused and that over 100 million children are engaged in hazardous work. Violence against children knows no geographic, ethnic, economic or cultural boundaries. It occurs in homes, in schools, on the street, in the workplace and in institutions. No country is immune.

We know that neglect, abuse, and violence have lifelong impacts on children. Those who experience violence at a young age are likely to die at an earlier age, to engage in risky behaviors, be more prone to alcoholism and drug abuse, and spend time incarcerated. With the burgeoning youth populations in Africa, this is a threat to the development gains being made across the continent and the stability and prosperity of the continent. Under the Action Plan's framework, we are facilitating the efforts of national governments and partners to prevent, respond to, and protect children from violence, exploitation, abuse, and neglect, including trafficking and child labor.

While the overall number of children experiencing violence, abuse, or neglect in Africa is not known, we can extrapolate from startling statistics. In the DRC, 64 percent of women have experienced physical violence since age 15 and 71 percent report some form of sexual, mental, or physical abuse by a spouse or partner. And of the more than 17,000 cases of rape reported in 2009, 58 percent of victims in reported sexual violence cases were under the age of 18. A UNICEF study in Swaziland, found that nearly one in four women experienced physical violence as children, one in three experienced sexual violence, and three in ten were emotionally abused. A similar study in Tanzania found that nearly three in ten women and one in seven men experienced sexual violence as children.

The U.S. Government takes part in Together For Girls, a public-private partnership, dedicated to ending violence against children, with a focus on sexual violence against girls. Using the U.S. Centers for Disease Control and Prevention's Violence Against Children Survey as an entry point, the partnership provides comprehensive data on the magnitude and consequences of sexual violence against children. The data gathered from the surveys provides the foundation for action, mobilizing countries to lead a response and inform solutions that are evidence-based.

Our programs provide safe spaces for children to heal and learn, giving parents and other caregivers time to address their own needs and those of their families. The programs also include outreach and direct support for parents, equipping them with the knowledge and skills needed to manage stress, support and care for their children and understand the impact of significant child protection risks such as family separation or child labor.

Since 2011, USAID's child protection work with UNICEF in the DRC has removed over 3,257 children associated with armed groups – including 202 girls – in North Kivu, South Kivu, Orientale, and Katanga provinces. We have provided separated children with temporary care in transit centers or foster families, supported their reintegration into their communities, and helped an additional 5,000 conflict-affected children to enroll in school or obtain vocational skills training. Additionally, we have strengthened the capacity of 15 local organizations assisting children associated with armed groups, and we have created or strengthened over 70 community committees to promote child rights at the grassroots level and prevent child recruitment into armed groups in the DRC.

Also in the DRC, we recently began implementation of a five-year program, the Appropriate Care for Families and Children program (SAFE from Soins Appropriés pour les Familles et les Enfants), that is strengthening services and systems to support family cohesion and respond to the separation of children. SAFE targets vulnerable children including child soldiers, street children, children accused of witchcraft, children involved in the legal system, children with disabilities, child laborers, and HIV/AIDS orphans. SAFE uses a community-based approach to help identify children at risk and reduce stigmatization, discrimination, and rejection through awareness campaigns and other behavior change strategies. Over five years, SAFE will directly benefit 7,000 children and 6,000 adults, and reach 40,000 community members through prevention and awareness-building activities.

Conclusion

Children living under conditions of serious physical deprivation or danger or who experience violence, abuse and neglect face fundamental threats to their survival, well-being, and future. If we do not focus on the child, we lose the person. Investments in a strong start for Africa's children are critical to laying a foundation for a healthy, productive future for Africa itself.

USAID remains committed to meeting the needs of vulnerable children in Africa while also addressing the root issues that create the conditions for conflict and abuse. Through our work in maternal and child health, nutrition, basic education, human rights, democratic governance, and humanitarian assistance we will continue tackle the underlying issues that lead to children's vulnerability. We look forward to our ongoing work across the U.S. Government – and with this Subcommittee – to promote healthy, resilient families and communities where children can thrive.

Thank you very much.

Mr. SMITH. Ambassador Jackson?

STATEMENT OF THE HONORABLE ROBERT P. JACKSON, PRINCIPAL DEPUTY ASSISTANT SECRETARY, BUREAU OF AFRICAN AFFAIRS, U.S. DEPARTMENT OF STATE

Ambassador JACKSON. Thank you, Mr. Chairman. And thank you for inviting me to testify on the Department of State's response to orphaned and vulnerable children in Africa.

This hearing is very timely, coming just weeks before the U.S.-Africa Leaders Summit on investing in the next generation.

The Department of State is committed to supporting children in adversity around the world, including orphaned and vulnerable children. This work is accomplished through the Department's diverse programmatic activities, diplomatic engagement, and policy development. We engage the expertise and capacity of multiple department offices and bureaus.

At the outset, I wish to make clear that the State Department does not isolate African orphans in its advocacy for children in adversity, nor does the Department relegate its concern only to Africa. All regional bureaus, many functional bureaus, and the leadership of the Department are focused on this. It is a very high priority. And we closely coordinate this work with USAID and other U.S. Government agencies.

Allow me to focus on some of the most prominent issues facing children in Africa, including AIDS, trafficking, and conflict, and how we are working in the Department and with our colleagues at USAID to help address these issues.

It is estimated that there are 17.8 million children who have lost one or both parents due to AIDS, and 90 percent of them live in sub-Saharan Africa. The President's Emergency Plan for AIDS Relief is addressing the needs of orphans and vulnerable children through programs that mitigate the social, emotional, and economic impacts of HIV/AIDS on children and reduce their risk and vulnerability while increasing their resilience.

These programs have kept children in school, maintained children in supportive family environments, kept children safe by working with governments to promote child-welfare system strengthening, including the prevention of child abuse, gender-based violence, and social protection, and reduced barriers to HIV and health and nutrition services, to name a few. Over the last 4 years, more than 5 million children worldwide have been supported by PEPFAR's orphans and vulnerable-children programs.

Second, conflicts in Africa, including those in the Central African Republic, Chad, the Democratic Republic of Congo, Cote d'Ivoire, Liberia, Nigeria, Sierra Leone, Somalia, South Sudan, Sudan, and Uganda, which you mentioned, have provoked an increase in the number of children recruited or used as child soldiers.

We take very seriously the issue of unlawful recruitment and use of children as soldiers in government or government-supported armed groups, as the Department is responsible for producing a list of these governments as mandated by the Child Soldier Prevention Act, CSPA.

In accordance with that act, we continue to work with African governments to address child soldiers in their countries, encouraging the signing and implementation of joint action plans with the U.N. Special Representative of the Secretary-General for Children and Armed Conflict.

We also support the work undertaken by UNICEF to demobilize, disarm, and rehabilitate former child soldiers. This year alone, UNICEF has secured the release of 1,000 child soldiers in the Central African Republic.

We have seen that these action plans can be effective. The actions taken by the Government of Chad to remove children from the armed-forces ranks were so successful that a verification mission undertaken by UNICEF found no child soldiers at all, and Chad was not listed this year on the CSPA list or the Annual Report of the Secretary-General on Children and Armed Conflict.

I have also seen firsthand how engaging with former child soldiers can make a difference. When I visited Liberia with Deputy Secretary of State Higginbottom in June, we met former child soldiers who had formed nongovernmental organizations and had created small businesses to help themselves and others reintegrate into society. One of these stressed the importance of healing, behavioral change, and economic opportunities, which underscored to me how crosscutting this issue is. Grassroots African efforts like this, people helping people, need to be encouraged and supported.

Third, we know children can be vulnerable to international and domestic human trafficking, whether through sex trafficking, forced child soldiering, or forced labor. AIDS orphans, including those from Swaziland and Lesotho, are particularly vulnerable to exploitation. Children throughout the continent are exploited in domestic servitude, forced begging, and forced labor in a variety of sectors, including mining, fishing, cattle herding, and harvesting coffee, cocoa, and rice. Armed conflict and other instability, poor economic conditions, food insecurity, rural poverty, and lack of social safety nets can also leave children vulnerable to trafficking in Africa.

Our Embassies in Africa do not just report on trafficking; they aggressively engage with governments and civil society, lobbying for anti-trafficking laws to be passed, for governments to prosecute traffickers, and for the protection of victims of trafficking, especially child victims.

Protection is a critical component of the United States' 3–P strategy for fighting trafficking in persons, the three P's being prosecution, protection, and prevention. Both the Africa Bureau and the Office to Monitor and Combat Trafficking in Persons fund victim-assistance programs that are designed specifically to respond to the comprehensive needs of child victims of trafficking. Beneficiaries are provided with safe and secure shelter, medical, paralegal, psychosocial counseling, and educational support. Furthermore, continuity of care is provided through ongoing case management and economic reintegration assistance to reduce the risk of re-trafficking.

One of the pillars of the U.S. Action Plan for Children in Adversity is strengthening families. When efforts to keep families together fail, domestic and international adoption may be one way to help children who have lost parents. Orphans constitute a large vulnerable population in Africa, and it is important for us to ensure that they are adopted in an ethical and transparent manner in accordance with international norms.

That is why we work with our Bureau of Consular Affairs to encourage countries to join and implement The Hague adoption convention to further ethical and transparent inter-country adoptions. Moreover, we have encouraged countries to align their child welfare systems and adoption practices with convention standards.

In conclusion, Mr. Chairman, through a range of activities, the Department of State works to support education, security, social, and child welfare systems to provide humanitarian assistance and to develop capacity for governance, rule of law, and the protection and advancement of human rights across the globe.

There are so many ways for us to help children in Africa, and it is important for us to work collaboratively to address the issue with a survivor-centered approach, pressing countries for laws to protect them, supporting efforts to implement those laws, and establishing protective services in conjunction with civil society. We look forward to continuing to work with our U.S. Government colleagues and with this subcommittee to address this important issue.

I would be pleased to take your questions, and I thank you very much.

Mr. SMITH. Thank you very much, Ambassador Jackson.

[The prepared statement of Mr. Jackson follows:]

Robert P. Jackson
Principal Deputy Assistant Secretary for the Bureau of African Affairs
U.S. Department of State

House Foreign Affairs Committee
Subcommittee on Africa, Global Health, Global Human Rights, and
International Organizations
July 16, 2014

"The Growing Crisis of Africa's Orphans"

Chairman Smith, Ranking Member Bass, and Members of the Committee,
Thank you for inviting me to testify on the Department of State's response to
orphaned and vulnerable children in Africa.

The Department of State is committed to supporting children in adversity around
the world, including orphaned and other vulnerable children. This work is
accomplished through the Department's diverse program activities, diplomatic
engagement, and policy development and engages the expertise and capacity of
multiple Department offices and bureaus. At the outset, I wish to make clear that
the State Department does not isolate African orphans in its advocacy for children
in adversity, nor does the Department relegate its concern only to Africa. All
regional bureaus, many functional bureaus, and the leadership of the Department
are focused on this; it is high priority. And we closely coordinate this work with
USAID and many other U.S. agencies. Allow me to focus on some of the most
prominent issues children in Africa face, including AIDS, trafficking, and conflict,
and how we are working here in the Department and with our colleagues at USAID
to help address these issues.

It's estimated that there are 17.8 million children that have lost one or both of their
parents due to AIDS, and 90 percent of those live in sub-Saharan Africa. PEPFAR
is addressing the needs of orphans and vulnerable children (OVC) through
programs that mitigate the social, emotional and economic impacts of HIV/AIDS
on children and reduce their risk and vulnerability while increasing their resilience.
These programs have kept children in school, maintained children in supportive
family environments, kept children safe by working with governments to promote
child welfare system strengthening (including prevention of child abuse, GBV, and
social protection), and reduced barriers to HIV and health and nutrition services, to

name a few. Over the last four years, more than five million children worldwide have been supported by PEPFAR OVC Programs.

Second, conflicts in the Central African Republic, Chad, the Democratic Republic of Congo, Cote d'Ivoire, Liberia, Sierra Leone, Somalia, South Sudan, Sudan, and Uganda have provoked an increase in the number of children recruited or used as child soldiers. We take very seriously the issue of unlawful recruitment and use of children as soldiers in government armed forces or government-supported armed groups as the department is responsible for producing a list of these governments as mandated by the Child Soldier Prevention Act (CSPA). In accordance with the CSPA, we continue to work with African governments to address child soldiers in their countries, including by encouraging the signing and implementation of joint action plans with the UN Special Representative of the Secretary General for Children and Armed Conflict (UNCAAC). We also support the work undertaken by UNICEF to demobilize, disarm and rehabilitate former child soldiers; this year alone UNICEF has secured the release of 1,000 child soldiers in the Central African Republic. We have seen that these action plans can be effective -- the actions taken by the Government of Chad to remove children from its ranks resulted in a verification mission undertaken with UNICEF last summer and fall, finding no child soldiers within the ranks of the Chadian National Army. Chad was subsequently not listed this year on the CSPA list or the Annual Report by the Secretary General on Children and Armed Conflict.

I have also seen first-hand how engaging with former child soldiers can make a difference. When I visited Liberia with Deputy Secretary of State Heather Higginbottom in June, we met former child soldiers who had formed non-governmental organizations and had created small businesses to help themselves and others re-integrate into society. One stressed the importance of healing, behavioral change and economic opportunities, which underscored to me how cross-cutting this issue is. Grassroots African efforts like this -- people helping people -- need to be encouraged and supported.

Third, we know children can be vulnerable to international and domestic human trafficking, whether through sex trafficking, forced child soldiering, or forced labor. AIDS orphans, including those from Swaziland and Lesotho, are particularly vulnerable to exploitation. Children throughout the continent are exploited in domestic servitude, forced begging, and forced labor in a variety of sectors, including mining, fishing, cattle herding, and harvesting coffee or rice. Armed conflict and other instability, poor economic conditions, food insecurity, rural poverty, and lack of social safety nets can also leave children vulnerable trafficking in Africa. Our embassies in Africa don't just report on trafficking, they aggressively engage with governments and civil society, pressing for anti-trafficking laws to be passed, for governments to prosecute traffickers and for protection of victims of trafficking, especially child victims.

Protection is a critical component of the USG "3-P" strategy for fighting trafficking in persons – prosecution, protection, prevention. Both the Africa Bureau and the Office to Monitor and Combat Trafficking in Persons fund victim assistance programs that are designed specifically to respond to the comprehensive needs of child victims of trafficking. Beneficiaries are provided with safe and secure shelter, medical, paralegal, psycho-social counseling, and educational support. Furthermore, continuity of care is provided through ongoing case management and economic reintegration assistance to reduce the risk of re-trafficking.

One of the pillars of the U.S. Action Plan for Children in Adversity is strengthening families. When efforts to keep families together fail, domestic and international adoption may be one way to help children who have lost parents. Orphans constitute a large, vulnerable population in Africa, and it is important for us to ensure that they are adopted in an ethical and transparent manner in accordance with international norms. This is why we work with our Bureau of Consular Affairs to encourage countries to join and implement The Hague Adoption Convention to further ethical and transparent inter-country adoptions. Moreover, we have encouraged countries to align their child welfare systems and adoption practices with Convention standards.

Conclusion

In conclusion, Mr. Chairman, through a range of activities the Department of State works to support education, security, social and child welfare systems; to provide humanitarian assistance; and to develop capacity for governance, rule of law, and the protection and advancement of human rights across the globe. There are so many ways for us to help children in Africa, and it is important for us to work collaboratively to address the issue with a survivor-centered approach: lobbying countries for laws to protect them, supporting efforts to implement those laws, and establishing protective services in conjunction with civil society. We look forward to continuing our work with our U.S. government colleagues and this subcommittee to address this important issue.

I would be pleased to take your questions and thank you very much.

Mr. SMITH. And let me just ask both of you, what are your time limitations? Again, we thought we would be in late last night, and then they unexpectedly ended the session, and now we have votes until about 3:45 p.m. What is your availability? Because I will ask some questions and risk missing the first vote. While you are figuring that out, I will just ask the first question.

Ms. Lindborg, you mentioned, and I thank you for your work on the first 1,000 days of life, from the moment of conception to the second birthday. As you may or may not know, I have worked on child survival since my first term in 1982—I got elected in 1980—and have worked on it ever since, every year offering amendments to increase, you know, vitamins, increase especially the issue of immunizations and oral-rehydration therapy for those suffering diarrheal disease, and all the rest. But we now know beyond any reasonable doubt those first 1,000 days of life are absolutely pivotal to a child, and I thank you for your work on that.

My question is, compared to other children in Africa, are the orphans disproportionately left out of programs that include the first 1,000 days of life, which would mean that they will be healthier, have a better immune system, or at least immunity capabilities, or are there very special efforts made to include them?

Secondly, you spoke about the failure to thrive. I remember being in Nicolae Ceausescu's orphanages right after his fall in Romania after being there many years, and all of a sudden we found 50 or 60 kids lined up, with one nurse or helper, and those kids were dying because they weren't even being picked up. And I am wondering if you could just maybe spend some time on the importance of, you know, this failure to thrive. I don't think enough people understand that.

And, Mr. Ambassador, my first question to you would be: The DR Congo, what is the glitch there? What does the administration do to try to reverse it? And how quickly can we expect any results? Do we think we will have results soon, especially for the families that are waiting so desperately to get their children and to begin bringing them home?

Ms. LINDBORG. Thank you.

On the efforts to include orphaned and vulnerable children, you know, there has been, fortunately, an important focus, through the efforts of this Action Plan for Children in Adversity, to make a special effort to reach out for orphans and vulnerable children.

One of the challenges that we have, especially in conflict settings, is we don't always know where they all are or how many there are. So one of the things that we have been doing is working with partners to improve our understanding of what is the pool of need, how to get a better understanding of who is not being included in the program. So that is an important ongoing development.

We also have a greater ability to target those who are orphans as a result of HIV/AIDS than those who are orphans through conflict or other means, simply because of the way that the funding is structured.

Finally, on the failure-to-thrive issue, I mean, this is really heartbreaking, and it has led us to really work hard on the second objective of trying to deinstitutionalize children and get them into more nurturing environments.

And there have been some very important successes on this. Like, for example, in Ethiopia, we have worked with the government. They did a review of all of their institutions, about 100 institutions, and they found that 45 of them were simply substandard. They closed them. And with USAID support, we worked to get those kids back into their families, in some instances, reunited, or with foster care or other places where they could get better care.

This is probably one of the areas where we need to spend the greatest additional focus. We are very determined to increase our ability to do these kind of programs. And the evidence is just overwhelming that you really have to take a whole-of-child approach.

So even as we have increased substantially our ability to feed children more nutritious food more effectively in those early days and work with pregnant and lactating women, we really need to keep focusing our attention on this second bit, on the failure-to-thrive issue.

Mr. SMITH. How is your time? And I know you have busy schedules.

Ms. LINDBORG. Well, I have a 3:30 that will be very hard to change.

Mr. SMITH. Okay. I understand.

And how about you?

Ambassador JACKSON. I am available, Mr. Chairman.

Mr. SMITH. You are? Thank you, Mr. Ambassador. If you could hold that then, and if I could ask you one other question. I have a dozen, but we are out of time on the floor.

I am the prime author of the Combating Autism Act. Started in 1997, it became law in 2000. Our reauthorization bill is pending over on the Senate side.

One of the things that the IACC Committee, headed up by NIH, found was that if women are getting folic acid 3 months before and they are getting prenatal vitamins, in other words, even before they think they might become pregnant, that the impact on both mother and child is significantly enhanced, and it mitigates the possibility—it is not de facto, they haven't proven it, but they believe it does—of the issue of autism and a whole lot of other maladies that could occur.

This is relatively new. And, you know, we have had hearings, we have another one in about a week or so, on autism globally here in our subcommittee.

And the question is, is there an understanding that reproductive health ought to be inclusive? Very often, it is seen as, you know, no babies, how does someone go about not having a child, rather than how do we enhance the prospects of a healthier mother and baby.

And now this new component of, if you start earlier, reproductive health, it means that your child is less likely to get autism. And tens of millions of Africans have autism, and it is an epidemic that parallels HIV/AIDS, but largely unrecognized and unfocused upon.

Your thoughts?

And when you are done with your comments, we will stand in recess, and I will have to read them. Be right back.

Ms. LINDBORG. So, first of all, thank you for, you know, your passion and commitment on these issues.

The focus of the first 1,000 days is very much about reproductive health issues and ensuring that you have healthy mothers and healthy babies, both tackling the issue of ending the preventable death of children under 5 and also ensuring that, through better science, through better ability to have access to healthcare services, through better nutrition, that we are able to continue to make gains in this realm.

So that is absolutely a strong focus through a whole variety of programs that we do that are focused on women who are in community situations as well as those who are in conflict environments where it becomes more difficult to provide those services but just as much of a priority.

Ambassador JACKSON. So, in terms of DRC adoptions, they were suspended last September due to the DRC Government's concerns about fraud, corruption, and potential child-buying and their lack of capacity to manage the adoption program.

We have been engaged continuously since then. We have met with Ministers of Foreign Affairs; Interior; Gender, Family and Children; and the Minister of Justice. On May 4th, Secretary Kerry met with President Kabila and made a personal plea for him to lift the suspension. Subsequent to that, we were able to secure exit permits for a small number of children.

Dr. Biden, the Second Lady of the United States, was in Kinshasa earlier this month. She also made a plea for new exit permits to be issued. And, this afternoon, some of my colleagues are meeting with the Congolese Ambassador at the State Department.

So my basic message is that we remain very engaged in attempting to secure exit permits for these children, while supporting the Congolese efforts to strengthen their own internal controls to assure that children are being adopted by families who will give them loving, caring homes.

[Recess.]

Mr. SMITH. The subcommittee will resume its sitting.

And I do want to welcome our distinguished witnesses and apologize profusely for that very long delay, which was attributable to votes. Like I said earlier, we thought that there were going to be a whole cluster last night and that we would have been relatively free today. That didn't happen, so I do apologize.

We are joined by Congressman Steve Stockman, who, frankly, just led a delegation to Abuja, to Nigeria, and he has freshly returned. And thank him for his leadership on these issues.

And I will now go to the introductions of our distinguished panelists, beginning first with Kelly Dempsey, who is the mother of three children, two of them adopted. She is an attorney, practicing primarily in adoption law in her own firm in North Carolina.

After overcoming her own struggle to bring home her daughter, adopted from Vietnam, her legal practice expanded from civil litigation to focus on immigration issues with the international adoptions of children living abroad. Ms. Dempsey has represented hundreds of families in dozens of countries to ensure that the adoption process was completed and they were able to return home with their children.

She also works to promote international adoption as a viable option for unparented children and to identify and implement solutions that enable more children to find permanent, loving homes.

We will then hear from Ms. Shimwaayi Muntemba, who is from Zambia and founded Zambia Orphans Aid in the United States. She was instrumental in the creation of the St. Peter Claver Society for African orphans at St. John's Catholic Church in Virginia.

She worked at the World Bank on Africa-related issues, such as microfinance, women's empowerment, and the environment and development balance. Indeed, it is because of her dedication to orphans affected by AIDS that she gave up her position at the World Bank to dedicate herself to this important cause.

We will then hear if from Ms. Jovana Jones, who is part of a military couple who are adopting a 5-year-old Congolese girl who is several hearing-impaired. Her adopted daughter is currently residing in a very poor orphanage, and while they are being billed for her medical expenses, she and her husband are unable to take her home with them. The prospects are limited for the Joneses' daughter if she is forced to stay in the DRC, and they are afraid for her life and wellbeing.

And, finally, we will hear from Muluemebet Chekol Hunegnaw, who is a senior director of Save the Children's global monitoring and evaluation and knowledge management unit. She is responsible for providing leadership for setting the vision and strategy of the monitoring and evaluation and the knowledge management system of its international programs in more than 50 countries.

She has more than 20 years of experience in international development and served as director of programs for the Africa region of Save the Children's South Sudan program. She also worked as a USAID mission monitoring and evaluation advisor in Ethiopia.

And I thank you again for your patience and look forward to your testimony.

If you could begin, Ms. Dempsey.

STATEMENT OF MS. KELLY DEMPSEY, GENERAL COUNSEL AND DIRECTOR OF ADVOCACY AND OUTREACH, BOTH ENDS BURNING

Ms. DEMPSEY. Thank you, Mr. Chairman. I first want to thank you for the opportunity to appear today before this subcommittee and to talk about an important tool of protection for the orphan child in Africa, and that specific tool is international adoption.

I have prepared a written statement, and I also ask that that be entered into the record.

Mr. SMITH. Without objection, it will be made a part of the record.

Ms. DEMPSEY. I am here on behalf of Both Ends Burning today, and we are a nonprofit advocacy organization dedicated to promoting and protecting every child's right to live in a permanent family.

Family is the bedrock of our society. There is nothing more important in a child's life than his or her connection to their parents. When that connection is threatened, we need our foreign policies to help strengthen it. When it is severed, it should be repaired. And when it can't be repaired, we should help form a new connection, and that connection should be formed through international or domestic adoption, when possible.

This is the central role, I think, of child protection and child welfare that is missing today in our foreign policies. Far too often, we relegate adoption to a simple immigration issue, and we are missing an opportunity to serve children well.

Department of State, through the Embassies in Addis Ababa and in Kinshasa, as well as the Office of Children's Issues, plays a key role in international adoptions. However, instead of aiding American families and advocating for orphaned children, the Department of State has become an obstacle that must be overcome in order for children to come home to their families. Instead of engaging the foreign governments in partnerships that promote permanency for children, the Department of State instead institutes policies that slow or stop adoptions. Instead of engaging the American adoptive parents, their adoption agencies, and advocate organizations, such as Both Ends Burning, we are regarded as adversaries. This approach is damaging children, and we have seen it over and over again.

I want to focus my remarks today on Ethiopia and the Democratic Republic of the Congo because those are the countries with which I have the most experience.

In Ethiopia, in 2010, we saw 2,500 children come home to the United States. It was an all-time high and just barely touching the need that exists in that country. What has happened since is a 60-percent decline.

And part of that is because, in 2010, when the growth was at an all-time high, the Department of State made the decision to try to close Ethiopia to adoptions. Luckily, there was resistance, and a team was sent in from USCIS and Department of State to investigate the problems that the Department of State believed existed in adoptions. And they reviewed more than 4,000 cases, all of the cases that had happened in the prior 2 years. And what that team found was that, overwhelmingly, these adoptions were good, ethical adoptions.

They found a cluster of factors, when present, that would warrant further investigation, and they found that cluster of factors to exist in about 5 percent of the cases. Everyone walked away believing that when those factors were present, adoptions would be looked at more closely to ensure ethical, transparent adoptions.

And, instead, what happened is the U.S. Embassy started putting files in a drawer. Instead of adjudicating cases, which is their mandate, they started putting files in a drawer. And what that meant for children is that they languished in an orphanage. They did not tell families, they did not tell USCIS, they did not tell the Ethiopian Government authorities; they simply put files in a drawer.

Time passed. Families banded together, as they often do. They reached out to Members of Congress because you all have become necessary players in the adoption process. And we are very grateful for the work you do. And what was discovered was that these cases weren't being adjudicated.

Another team went over from USCIS, and they conducted a review of those cases, and, in the end, all but one was approved. But what that cost families and children was anywhere from an extra 6 months to 1 year of their life, extraordinary financial expenses, and the emotional toll that cannot be repaid. And what has happened since then has been an astonishing chilling effect on international adoptions from Ethiopia—again, a 60-percent decline since the high of 2,500 in 2010.

Similarly, in the Democratic Republic of the Congo, we saw a period of growth. In 2010, there were 41 adoptions, and that number has slowly increased over the last few years.

In 2013, unable to handle the influx of cases, several hundred, the Department of State, again, began seeking ways to slow or stop adoptions from the Democratic Republic of the Congo. They implemented a policy of 100-percent mandatory field investigations despite the fact that over 97 percent of all cases coming out of Democratic Republic of the Congo had been approved. So that is a 3-percent denial. I would say it doesn't justify the allocation of resources.

And what they told families and what they told the Democratic Republic of the Congo was that that would lengthen the adoption process but it would ensure integrity, which we certainly all support. However, there was no increase in the allocation of resources, and, instead, there were unsubstantiated allegations of fraud.

Shortly thereafter, the suspension that now exists went into place, and over 800 families became stuck in a process and over 800 children became stuck in orphanages, unable to come home to their families.

And what we saw immediately following the suspension was, frankly, not much. The Department of State, instead of becoming advocates for these families and their children, instead of sharing their experiences of 90-percent approvals, began to sit quietly and to encourage the families to do the same. More than 10 months passed, and, still, families are not getting answers to their questions.

In April, recognizing the size of this crisis and the lack of response from the Department of State, Both Ends Burning became engaged in an advocacy campaign and Congress became engaged in an advocacy campaign. And we have had tremendous support, both from you and from this subcommittee and from the entire House, and we are very grateful for House Resolution 588 that was recently passed.

It is not enough to bring these children home. And so the families—I would like to acknowledge the ones that are here today. In addition to Ms. Jones, who will speak, we have families who are here.

I also have affidavits from six of the families that I would like to be entered into the record, as well.

Mr. SMITH. Without objection, so ordered.

Ms. DEMPSEY. Thank you.

And what we learned from their affidavits and from these families is that there has been a total lack of response, a total lack of urgency, and a total lack of meaningful engagement to resolve this crisis.

We ask for urgency to move forward in this and that we find a solution that allows these kids to come home before any more die.

We are aware of 10 that have perished during the wait, and we believe that many more will. In fact, one of the affidavits——

Mr. SMITH. Perished from what?

Ms. DEMPSEY. From waiting. I mean, dehydration, malaria, malnutrition, easily avoidable diseases, when they could have been home in this country.

We have had siblings separated, biological siblings separated, due to errors at the Embassy. One kid is home; one kid is stuck in Congo waiting for processing and the suspension to lift. Really astonishing and outrageous tragedies that could and should be avoided.

And so what I think is of paramount importance and what Both Ends Burning is advocating for and asking for is a foreign policy solution that creates a tool by which permanency can become a central tenet of child welfare and child protection.

When I listened to the speakers earlier today, I didn't hear that. And, in fact, I didn't hear anybody talking about finding family solutions for kids when their own families and kinship care wasn't available.

It shouldn't be relegated to a last-place idea. It should be planned for and advocated for so that children are getting their most basic needs met. And, today, in the Department of State, through the Office of Children's Issues and Consular Affairs, it simply isn't happening.

I would be happy to answer any questions.

Mr. SMITH. Thank you so very much for that testimony, disturbing, extremely disturbing, as it is. And we will get to questions when our other panelists are concluded, but I thank you for that.

[The prepared statement of Ms. Dempsey follows:]

Testimony of Kelly Tillotson Dempsey,
General Counsel and Director of Advocacy and Outreach, Both Ends Burning
Before the House Subcommittee on Africa, Global Health, Global Human Rights, and International
Organizations
July 16, 2014

Thank you Chairman Smith, Ranking Member Engel, Subcommittee Members, and Subcommittee Staff Members for the opportunity to testify at this important hearing on the African Orphan. I am here today to talk about one important tool of protection for African orphans -- international adoption. It is an honor to be invited to appear before you and to have my testimony considered as you develop strategies to assist the millions of children living outside of family care in Africa.

I appear today on behalf of Both Ends Burning (BEB), a non-profit organization committed to protecting and promoting every child's right to a permanent loving family. We are funded strictly through private philanthropy. We have no ties, financial or otherwise, to adoption agencies, adoptive families, religious or other organizations. We work solely on behalf of children around the world who are in desperate need of permanent loving families.

Both Ends Burning believes in permanency for children. We believe there is no connection more important in this world than a child's connection to his or her parents. We believe that when threatened, that connection needs to be strengthened; when severed, it needs to be repaired; and when it is not possible or not in the best interests of the child to repair that connection, that a new parental connection needs to be made. We believe every child in this world has a basic human right to be raised in a permanent loving family, and for children who cannot be raised in their birth family; adoption is the most appropriate solution.

I come to this work as a Mom to three children, two adopted, one from Vietnam and one domestically, so I know firsthand the issues that present themselves in adoption. In fact, my personal experience being stuck in Vietnam with my daughter Ada shifted my career focus from litigation to adoption. In private practice, I have been honored to represent hundreds of families seeking to adopt from all over the world, most of whom reach me when their efforts to bring home their adopted child run into a barrier that results in their child becoming stuck in the adoption process. The overwhelming majority of the time, that barrier is the Department of State.

What I've learned over the years is that Members of Congress have become a necessary participant in international adoptions. On many occasions I have accompanied families to your offices when no other avenue was available to a child stuck in a political or regulatory quagmire. We've come to you time and time again to seek your assistance, often when the Department of State fails to help or advocate for children and their families. More and more it seems there is a step in the process of adoption that requires the intervention of a Member of Congress, or as we are seeing now in the Democratic Republic of Congo (DRC), the entire Congress, in order to get children into their permanent families. We have almost gotten to the point where adoption agencies should place contact information for Members of Congress in the orientation materials they provide to prospective adoptive parents. While we are very grateful to Members of Congress, this is not how the process of adopting a child should work.

We all agree that every child needs and deserves a family. The Hague Convention on the Protection of Children and Cooperation in Respect of Intercountry Adoption (Hague Convention), the UN Convention on the Rights of the Child, and other international instruments recognize that the family is the fundamental unit of society and that every child should be able to grow up in a family. Indeed, this

Subcommittee and the House of Representatives recently acknowledged this truth in passing House Resolution 588, making it clear that a child's right to a family is a basic human right that warrants protection.

In Africa, there is staggering need. Although calculating and defining orphans is difficult, it is estimated that there are nearly 50 million orphans in Africa. There are about 5 million orphans in Ethiopia and another 4 million in the DRC. At least 12% of all children in Sub-Saharan Africa are orphans, most due to war, AIDS/HIV, malaria, cholera, and famine. From 1990 to 2000 the number of orphans in Africa rose by 34%, a rate of increase that has not showed any signs of slowing down, much less being reversed. We must bring forward solutions that prioritize families for these vulnerable children, and adoption must be seen as such a solution.

With the implementation of The Hague Convention in 2008, the Office of Children's Issues, which previously had responsibility for issuing orphan visas for adopted children, was designated as our new Central Authority for Adoptions. It was the expectation of many Members of Congress that this would improve adoption systems and increase the number of children being adopted. However, adoptions have declined by 69% over the last nine years and the Department of State has simply continued in its primary role as gatekeeper. To be successful, international adoption must be seen as much more than an immigration issue, and there must be a true sense of urgency in our government's actions as adoptions are processed.

The Department of State, through its embassies and the Office of Children's Issues, plays a key role in international adoptions by U.S. citizens. Yet, rather than serving to aid families trying to navigate the complex process of international adoption or advocate for children in need, the Department of State stands as an impediment. Instead of engaging foreign governments in partnerships that promote ethical domestic and international adoptions and permanency for children, the Department of State institutes policies programs to slow or stop adoptions that are premised on mistrust and suspicion. In so doing, it both fails to do the positive work that we were all hoping our Central Authority would do in helping to encourage child permanency and it goes far beyond its statutory authority. The Department's demonstrated bias against adoption is damaging children and preventing children from finding permanent loving homes here in the United States. My professional experience has allowed me to witness this first hand in both Ethiopia and DRC.

Both Ethiopia and DRC had recent periods of strong growth in international adoptions, due mainly to the extraordinary need in both countries but also because so many other countries, such as Nepal and Vietnam, had closed. However, today adoptions from Ethiopia are drastically declining and adoptions from DRC are in crisis.

ETHIOPIA

Ethiopia Adoption Stats	2010	2011	2012	2013	Total
RFEs issued	unknown	19	51	53	123
NOIDs issued	unknown	16	8	18	42
Denials/Revocations	unknown	39	32	38	109
Approved Adoptions	2511	1732	1567	993	6803

No one disputes that there is enormous need in Ethiopia. As more and more Americans learned about the need of these children and the possibility to provide a family to a child from Ethiopia, they began to do so. The adoption program grew and thousands of orphan children began finding loving homes in the United States.

However, rather than regarding the growth of adoptions in Ethiopia as a success, the Department of State chose to view the program as problematic for two main reasons: 1) it could not properly handle the caseload and did not receive additional resources; and 2) Consular Officers are trained to look upon all immigration, including orphan visas, with suspicion and doubt.

As the program grew, the US Embassy in Addis Ababa and the Department of State in Washington started issuing public warnings about the weaknesses of the Ethiopian adoption system. Such warnings are a frequently-used tactic by the Department of State when an adoption program experiences growth, and had recently been used to justify closure of adoptions in Nepal. Both Ends Burning recently issued an investigative report on Department of State's conduct in closing Nepal, entitled Paper Chains, and I have brought a summary of this report to share with you today should you be interested in learning more. By the end of 2010, when adoptions from Ethiopia were at an all-time high, the Department of State began to advocate for the closure of the Ethiopian adoption program, just as it had done in Nepal.

In response, in January 2011, a small team of investigators from USCIS and Department of State traveled to Addis Ababa to review the adoption program. The team conducted a comprehensive review of information about every adoption processed from Addis Ababa in the preceding two years-- some 4,000 cases. The team made a public report in April of that year finding that the allegations made by the Department of State simply were not true. Instead of finding rampant fraud and a broken system of adoptions, they found that the vast majority of the cases were ethical adoptions of legal orphans. In fact, not one single case had been denied based on a finding of fraud according to their review.

The review revealed that inconsistencies in the paperwork were the product of careless errors or poor record keeping, problems that should reasonably be expected in a developing nation. The investigation also identified a small subset of factors that, when present in a case, could justify further investigation by the US Embassy in Addis and recommended that the Embassy focus its investigative resources accordingly. In the end, the joint decision was made to continue the Ethiopian adoption program and the US Embassy promised that, going forward, it would immediately transfer cases with material inconsistencies or discrepancies to the USCIS Field Office in Nairobi and that it would return any 1600 submissions that were incomplete or had errors to the adoption service providers.

Inexplicably, in the face of this good news, the U.S. Embassy ignored the team's findings and continued to insist on lengthy field investigations and require families to jump through additional hoops, such as submitting new translations for documents with insignificant errors. And they started putting select cases in a drawer instead of approving them, apparently because they felt there was something problematic in the cases. However, they did this quietly and without telling the adoptive parents, the adoption service providers, USCIS, Ethiopian authorities, or anyone at all.

The Department of State can legally do one of two things when reviewing an orphan petition: 1) they can approve the case; or 2) they can find the case "not clearly approvable" and send it to U.S. Citizenship and Immigration Services (USCIS) for further review. Orphan petitions are also entitled to priority treatment at U.S. Embassies, and simply setting a file in a drawer is a violation of the obligations the U.S. Embassy has to the American citizens it serves. However, in 2011, the US Embassy in Addis was not treating these cases as a priority or forwarding the cases to USCIS as not clearly approvable. Instead they were piling cases up in a drawer. Under mounting pressure, they started telling some of the families that their cases had been forwarded to USCIS even though they had not.

In September 2011, USCIS was getting irate calls from waiting families and became aware of the drawer full of cases in the US Embassy in Addis. In response, a team of four USCIS officers went to Ethiopia in November to resolve the outstanding cases. This team spent two weeks working at the U.S. Embassy processing the "65 drawer cases" in the infamous "Addis Review Room." In the end, all but one of these cases were approved, and the one case that was denied was not denied due to a finding of fraud. However, the actions of the US Embassy caused children to remain in an orphanage for up to a year longer than was necessary.

Both Ends Burning has reviewed the cases that were stuck in the drawer in Addis Ababa and has interviewed these American families. In so doing, we discovered alarming trends in the tactics employed by U.S. Embassy staff during their investigations. Birth parents reported being intimidated, misled, and repeatedly asked confusing questions in an attempt to coerce contradictory statements. Birth parents also report instances of being deceived by US Embassy staff, including one birth father being told that his son was only being adopted so his kidneys could be harvested. In the end, no fraud was found and the US Embassy's concerns were proven untrue. It remains a mystery who instructed the US Embassy in Addis Ababa to begin the secret segregation of these cases or why, but the effects on the families and their children were terrible. Moreover, the effect on Ethiopian adoptions was chilling. Since the drawer debacle, fewer Ethiopian orphans are finding their way into American homes each year, despite enormous and increasing need. This trend can and should be reversed.

Democratic Republic of Congo

DRC Adoption Stats	2010	2011	2012	2013	Total
RFEs issued	unknown	1	35	114	150
NOIDs issued	unknown	4	0	2	6
Denials/Revocations	unknown	3	7	12	22
Approved	41	133	240	311	725

There are over 4 million orphans in the DRC. One in seven children dies before reaching the age of five. Children, in particular orphaned and abandoned children, are at risk of being trafficked, victims of sexual abuse, or forced to become child soldiers or mine workers. Against this backdrop of devastation and destitution hundreds of American families chose to adopt children from the DRC. Over the last four years more and more American families looking to adopt were drawn to the DRC and more and more children from the DRC were being provided with a permanent, loving home. And then, as had happened before in Nepal, Ethiopia, and other countries, the U.S. Embassy in Kinshasa became concerned about the "explosive" growth (from a handful to several hundred) of adoptions in the DRC and their ability to handle the increased workload.

In response, the Embassy decided to implement mandatory field investigations for all cases. This new requirement was designed to slow the flow of adoptions. A process that had taken families a couple of weeks to complete now takes, on average, more than six months to complete. This requirement alone has more than doubled the length of the adoption process at the very time in a child's life that expedience is essential. To be clear, an increase in field investigations or even a requirement that every case undergo a field investigation may be warranted if there is evidence of corruption or fraud that necessitates such a measure. However, in the DRC, such a radical policy does not appear to be supported by the numbers, and based on the timing of the suspension, may well have been a factor in the DRC's decision to suspend adoption exit letters.

Today, though adoptions continue to proceed through the courts in DRC, adopted children are unable to come home to their adoptive parents due to the suspension on exit letters put in place by the Government of the Congo in September 2013. Through my work at Both Ends Burning, I have had the honor and privilege of working with hundreds of the families caught in this crisis. Both Ends Burning has undertaken an advocacy campaign to bring this issue to the attention of Congress and the general public, in hopes that your direct involvement will lead to a resolution. I am proud to report that your efforts to date have brought 21 adopted Congolese children home to the United States; however hundreds more are still waiting, including some very critically ill children that are unlikely to survive the wait. I am hopeful that this crisis can be ended with your continued support, engagement, and oversight.

According to the DRC government, this suspension arises from concerns over the integrity of their adoption process and the welfare of the children once they leave DRC for their new homes. We acknowledge that these concerns may be valid, and we believe DRC has the absolute right and obligation to ensure its children are truly orphans and will be safe and loved by their adoptive families. We also know that our government is capable of addressing and overcoming these concerns through direct dialog and engagement, and could easily share its findings of approval for 97% of the adoptions it processes. The Department of State could and should have been actively involved from the moment the suspension went into effect to find a solution. Nearly 800 American families are impacted by the suspension, and children are dying waiting to come home from avoidable maladies such as dehydration, malnutrition and malaria. This is a true crisis, as you well know, and one that I believe could have been avoided and can be ended.

The Department of State's decision to implement mandatory field investigations in 100% of the cases was an underlying reason that the DRC had concerns over the integrity of the process. However, mandatory field investigations were not implemented to test the integrity of the system, but instead to slow the growth of DRC adoptions. This policy has served to take what had been a fairly quick adoption process and double its length. The Department of State hoped a longer more complex process would discourage American families from initiating new adoptions in DRC.

With so few cases ending in denial, and no indication that the denials were the product of fraud, one must question the reason for a policy mandating that 100% of the cases be subjected to field investigations. This extraordinary use of Embassy resources, and the attendant delay suffered by children waiting to come home, runs counter to serving the orphan children of Africa. However, assuming that field investigations in 100% of the cases is necessary, more resources should be allocated by the Department of State and USCIS to process a pipeline that today represents more than 10% of international adoptions by Americans worldwide. There is simply no reason a child should remain in an orphanage while the Department of State waits for cases to pile up to justify travel to remote regions, or to make time to place a phone call to an orphanage. The Department of State and USCIS should immediately send more staff to process the pipeline in DRC.

In addition to needlessly creating new hurdles and extraordinary delays, the U.S. Embassy in Kinshasa and the Department of State have failed to adequately serve American families and their children during this crisis. The Department of State has not been transparent and responsive to the families' requests for information. Until very recently, the Department of State did not appear to be meaningfully engaged in trying to end the crisis. For example, it took the Department of State more than seven months to determine how many families were impacted by the suspension. Without knowing the demography of the American families, or the children they are seeking to adopt, the Department of State cannot reasonably be expected to have been effective in advocating on their behalf.

One of the primary justifications given by the DRC for their suspension has been their concern for fraud and trafficking. In order to understand this concern, many families have frequently asked how many cases of fraud the US Embassy has found and the consistent answer has been that the Department of State does not know. This inability to provide accurate basic information is unfortunately not limited to questions about fraud in adoptions.

Adoptive American families have experienced unanticipated and unnecessary delays. Some have gone months without receiving answers to specific questions, whether in person, by phone, or in emails. Several families have been told that it would be months before their field investigations could possibly be completed or, in some cases, even started. Families have been told to "choose another country" or terminate their adoptions and relinquish their already adopted children. One family was even asked by an embassy Consul if they thought that Americans were beginning to see that adoption from the DRC was too difficult and hence they should look elsewhere. Both Ends Burning has collected affidavits from families who want to share their experiences with you, and a quick review of these sworn statements reveals a fundamental failure of the Department of State to appropriately respond to this crisis.

CONCLUSION

We can and must do better. Improving the situation however requires, at a minimum, a restructuring of responsibilities at the Department of State. The Office of Children's Issues and the Bureau of Consular Affairs is not the appropriate home for child welfare and child permanency issues. Their charter is too narrow in scope and they start at "no" in adjudicating adoption cases, believing their primary job is to find fraud. They lack expertise in facilitating ethical adoptions, and child permanency is not consistent with their primary responsibilities. Adoption is much more than a simple immigration matter and we must promulgate a foreign policy that does more for orphan children in need. In the last nine years we have seen a 69% decline in international adoptions, and the policies and practices of the Department of State are, in part, responsible.

A child's right to a family should be a central focus of the Department of State. Advocacy for child permanency must become a fundamental tenet of US foreign policy. To ensure the right of each child to a family and to further the principle of child permanency, responsibility for inter-country adoption policy and case administration should be moved from the Under Secretary for Management; with the exception of functions that need to be performed in US Embassies, such as investigations and orphan visa issuance.

We recommend the creation of an Office or Bureau reporting to the Under Secretary for Civilian Security, Democracy and Human Rights focused upon child permanency. This new organization should work closely with children's programming within USAID and the US Government's Action Plan for Children in Adversity. The leader of this organization should also be actively engaged with promoting the right of every child to a family as an active part of our foreign policy. In addition, we propose that the leader of the new office be subject to Senate confirmation, providing an important check-and-balance to ensure that the person in charge is both qualified in child permanency issues and focused on the needs of children globally.

Both Ends Burning supports the Children In Families First (CHIFF) Act (H.R. 4143) which incorporates provisions such as those described above. We strongly encourage the Foreign Affairs Committee to consider this legislation and the benefits that would accrue from its enactment.

There is great opportunity to provide meaningful interventions in Africa that will fulfill every child's right to a family. Thank you for your commitment to this right. I am happy to answer any questions you may have.

Mr. SMITH. Ms. Muntemba?

STATEMENT OF SHIMWAAYI MUNTEMBA, PH.D., FOUNDER, ZAMBIA ORPHANS OF AIDS

Ms. MUNTEMBA. Good afternoon. I am a Zambian citizen, as the chair has said, who has personally been touched by the orphan problem, having lost 5 younger sisters and brothers, leaving a total of 11 children, some as young as 3 and 5.

The good thing is that my nieces and nephews have helped me appreciate the orphan phenomenon and have spurred me to both focus on HIV and AIDS and social protection as part of my work and to be proactive in seeking assistance to reach those orphans whose families cannot provide for them adequately.

We have heard that there are 56 million orphans in Africa, but this is an official figure. In Africa, official numbers do not capture all orphans. Many deaths occur in rural areas, and these are not recorded.

The definition of ''orphans'' has also distorted their numbers. For example, to UNAIDS, an orphan should have lost both parents and is under 15 years of age. UNICEF'S definition embraces children zero to 17 years old who have lost one or both parents. African governments have adopted this definition.

With so many armed conflicts raging in Africa, some civil society institutions—and I tend to agree with them—are advocating the definition to include abandoned and alone children. And these are many in most of the countries in central and western Africa.

On the causes, we can identify five major causes of orphanhood in Africa: Armed and civil conflict, natural disasters, weak and unequal health systems, abject poverty, and HIV and AIDS.

I have been asked to say a few words on HIV and AIDS. HIV and AIDS has hit eastern and southern Africa the hardest. Seventy percent of Africa's 15.1 million orphans of AIDS are in the eastern and southern subregions, most of them in the southern.

But southern Africa reports the highest uptick of antiretroviral treatment in Africa. It leads national governmental budgetary allocations to HIV and AIDS. Yet, in 2012, more infections and AIDS-related deaths occurred in this subregion. Orphan numbers have risen exponentially in the last 2 decades and are poised to grow over the next few years and decades.

The question is, why is this? I suggest that interventions seem to focus disproportionately on treatment and away from prevention. The gender dimension of HIV and AIDS and its treatment and the generational unequal access to treatment are impacting negatively on AIDS management outcomes. As well, poverty is undermining the effectiveness of treatment among the majority poor in most of our countries.

A look at the impact on orphans: Children are firstly hit emotionally, as we have heard. When AIDS is the cause of death, stigma affects younger children within their communities and at school. Children have lost educational opportunities either because caregiving families are too poor or are not near schools.

Another impact has been that of abuse in hosting families. In such situations, girls are treated as indentured labor and/or sex objects.

Another is the phenomenon of child-headed households, some heads as young as 7 years old but many around 10 and 11. Those heads who contract HIV are hardly on treatment.

Response: I wish to focus on two groups, close or extended family members. Initially, they responded positively, but as orphan numbers grew alongside entrenched poverty, families became overwhelmed. Today, many extended families have difficulties taking on that responsibility. And this is why I am very much touched by what is being tried in the way of adoptions. What was normal in our cultures in Africa has become a burden to many.

Second, within the international community, Africans in the diaspora have responded by mobilizing financial and technical support in the countries where they live and work. I will give two examples from the Washington area.

In 2000, supported by former Ambassadors and Embassy staff in Zambia and other African countries, we formed Zambia Orphans of AIDS, now Zambia Orphans Aid. We now operate in the UK as well and are registered in Zambia. Through community-based organizations and community schools, we have reached over 10,000 orphans—a drop in the ocean, perhaps.

In 2004, St. John Catholic Church in McLean, Virginia, formed the St. Peter Claver Society for African Orphans. Through four institutions in Kenya and Zambia, the Society has assisted many orphans in Kenya and Zambia over the last 10 years, offering them the means for HIV testing, for being looked after by physiotherapists, for access to education, and for general food and nutritional needs.

In both cases, individual Americans have rallied in support of the orphans. But I must underline, though, that despite the goodwill and hard work, the demand outstrips the supply. What then, Mr. Chairman?

Previous contributions from him and probably from her may offer some of what we have to look at. But I feel that there are other opportunities for a minimum humanitarian response.

Number 1) greater political will is needed at the national level on behalf of orphans.

Number 2) higher-education funds are needed for orphans, to include technical and entrepreneurial skills training, specifying a proportion for girls.

Number 3) cash and in-kind support for child-headed families need to be intensified, but—and I underline this—for a specified timeframe, after which alternative care options must have been identified and offered to the children. However, this support must be flexible enough to respond to the shifting orphan care priorities.

I thank you for offering me the opportunity.

Mr. SMITH. Ms. Muntemba, thank you so much for your testimony.

[The prepared statement of Ms. Muntemba follows:]

Testimony of Dr. Shimwaayi Muntemba
Founder, Zambia Orphans Aid
Subcommittee on Africa, Global Health, Global Human Rights, and International
Organizations
The Growing Crisis of Africa's Orphans
July 16, 2014

African Orphans, Causes and Impact

"If all orphans formed a country of their own, it would be among the 10 largest nations in the world"[1.] Indeed, at figures ranging between 150 M (UNAIDS) and 153 M (UNICEF; UNHCR)[2], that country would be the world's 9th largest, ahead of the Russian Federation. At 56 M the Orphans' country in Africa would be the fourth largest after Nigeria, Ethiopia and the Democratic Republic of Congo.[3]

This submission sets out to explore the phenomenon of orphans: who constitutes an orphan; why are there so many orphans in Africa proportionate to the Continent's population, what and who are the major drivers of orphanhood? We shall attempt to understand what it means to be an orphan. In examining the impacts of orphanhood on the affected children, we shall consider the many ways orphans themselves respond and react to the loss of parents. We shall examine the responses from family, including extended, the community and community based organizations, national and international non-governmental organizations, faith- based institutions, national governments and the international community. We shall explore how best to respond to this phenomenon, especially from the orphans' perspectives.

Definition of an orphan. To many people, an orphan is a child whose both parents have died. The Joint United Nations Programme on HIV/AIDS (UNAIDS) understands orphan to mean a child under 15 years. To the United Nations Children's Fund (UNICEF) on the other hand orphan refers to a child under 18 who would have lost one or both parents. Hence they coined the phrase 'single' or 'double' orphans. In some African societies, a child becomes an orphan when both parents or the mother dies. This has caused confusion in orphan numbers, as indicated above especially when key agencies hold different interpretations. In the last few years, the international community and African governments have adopted UNICEF's interpretation.

Some institutions interested in children fleeing conflict situations have put a case for broadening orphanhood to include children who are 'alone'.[4] When communities are forced to flee their homes, at night and at gun point many children get disengaged from their parents. They find themselves all alone. Take the case of Nyagonar, a 10 years old South Sudanese girl. Her father was shot in front of their house. The mother took her daughter and run for refuge in the woods. Four days later when things appeared to have calmed down, they went back to their house, only to be woken up at night by gunshots in the compound. The girl recalls how everyone ran out of their houses. In the dark, she lost her mother. She ran on with the others,

as shots could be heard from everywhere. When she got to the UNHCR shelter, she looked for her mother but could not find her, "I never saw her again", she lamented. Weeks later, with others, she left on foot on a two months journey to Pagak, a refugee camp 300 km away. "I only want my mother and to go back home. I have nobody else" she often cried.[5]
In May 2014, the United Nations Office for the Coordination of Humanitarian Affairs reported of one UN camp that at a single time sheltered 4,000 children.[6]

Ten years after the end of armed conflict in Liberia, children who had been taken to a refugee camp in Ghana still lived there. In 2008, Andy Jones founded Heartwood Orphan Home in Liberia and moved the children there in 2010. In 2014, the children remain unclaimed and alone.[7] The UNHCR has a long process that leads such children to gain orphan status. But, do they not deserve the orphan status from when they find themselves alone?
This submission confines itself to the officially designated orphans. However, there is a strong case for broadening the concept of an orphan, for indeed the many orphans like Nyagonar, alone and desperate, could be in as sad a situation as the accepted orphans. Numbers of orphans globally rise to 160 M if abandoned and alone children are included.[8]

Causes of orphanhood: In Africa, we could identify five major causes of this phenomenon-- armed and civil conflict, AIDS, weak or non functioning health systems, natural disasters, and abject poverty.
Armed and civil conflict: During the last two decades, 25 countries in Africa have experienced armed conflict. Fourteen experience on- going conflicts in 2014. West and Central Africa have been ridden by lengthy armed conflicts that have left many soldiers and civilians dead or maimed. Majority of their estimated 22.1 M orphans in 2012 are a result of conflicts.
One country in West Africa will demonstrate the dire effects of internal armed conflict; one case in Eastern Africa will show how ethnicity can play a negative instead of positive role for children; and two examples in West Africa will prove how power structures, ethnicity and religion create civil conflict and orphans.

We read about the many atrocities committed against civilians in rural **Sierra Leone** in the late 1990s to early 2000s when the pro and anti- government forces let out their anger on civilians: men were killed in front of their families, women raped in front of their children, families separated as some were killed and others, especially women, taken by soldiers to act as carriers and 'bush wives.' Children were captured, boys as soldiers, girls as sex objects, while others were left to fend for themselves. Survivors have told stories of how, later, the child soldiers, some as young as 8, terrorized captured women and other children. Children who did not manage to get away were killed, but those who got away wandered the countryside without parents or adult family members. Some managed to reach the 'safety' of the capital city, Freetown, where they ended up on its streets. Others found their way to refugee camps in neighboring countries, as unaccompanied minors.[9]

We read and watch documentaries about the horrors of the 1994 **Rwanda** genocide. Here, too, children were separated from their parents. Memories of what happened lived in the consciousness of many children, some babies at the time, for a long time. Some of the raped women carried and gave birth to children they grew to hate because of what they reminded them of. These women were known in their communities as having been raped and worse as having carried the children of those who perpetrated the massacres. They were shunned; their children were not only hated by their mothers but also held in contempt in their communities and schools, while other children avoided them. Their households did not get any help from funds the Government allocates to assisting orphans in the households where they live.[10] This outcome of soldier abuse of sex as a weapon of war may be observed in other countries with conflict experiences (Sierra Leone and the Democratic Republic of Congo, as examples).

Many African countries have experienced brutalities from State security forces. Citizens have resorted to demonstrations as the only non violent way to express their discontent. In many cases, these have resulted in deaths as armed forces opened fire on them A case in point is **Guinea** where after protracted politically driven conflict, citizens resorted to demonstrations. Since 2010 and as recent as May, 2012, these have been brutally put down. Guns have been fired indiscriminately into crowds, killing many adults who left orphans behind. Ethnic and religious battles have also taken their toll in the country.[11] But perhaps Nigeria has the best known and most devastating civil conflicts.

In **Nigeria**, conflicts have taken many forms: armed ethnic- driven conflicts, and conflicts in the Niger Delta where both government organs and oil companies have unleashed weapons of destruction on the communities who have protested over many issues, from environmental damage to some share in the proceeds. Over the years, many people have been killed during protests. The military has been used to suppress communities, and they have been accused of house/village burnings and thousands of killings. Some reports have put deaths of civilians in the Niger Delta to about 1,000 each year since 1994.[12] The present Government has a more democratic stance, giving citizens of the Delta Region some hope for peace. Nigeria has also suffered from religious-based conflicts. The North in particular has been in the news in the last few years with regard to religious- driven strife: villages and schools have been burned, people and school children killed and/or kidnapped. It is not surprising, therefore, that in 2012, Nigeria was home to 11.5 M orphans. Only 2M of them were orphans of AIDS.[13]

HIV and AIDS:

AIDS and Orphans, 2012, by region (millions)

Region	Living with HIV/AIDS		New infections		Deaths		AIDS orphans		Orphans all causes		Total population
Global	35.3		2.3		1.6		17.8		150.0		1393.7
Sub-Saharan Africa	25.0	71%	1.6	70%	1.2	75%	15.1	85%	56.0	37%	913.1
West-Central Africa			-		-		4.4	12%	28.1	-	441.5
East & Southern Africa			-		-		10.6	30%	27.9	-	149.7
Southern Africa			-		-		6.04	17%	-	-	-

Source: UNAIDS reports

The above table shows that AIDS is the single largest driver of orphans in the Eastern and Southern sub-regions, Southern Africa contributing a larger portion.

There is no definitive cause of the above situation in Southern (and Eastern) Africa. Many reasons have been advanced: societal tolerance of multiple partners, urbanization, inter country migration particularly to South Africa which at 17.9% has the third highest prevalence rate in the sub-region, higher levels of sex workers, a strong network of men. Existence of a more portent HIV restricted to the sub-region. The fact remains that this sub-region has experienced higher levels of infection and deaths. While the prevalence rates have been going down, the rates in most countries in the sub-region remain between 10% and 15%, one country recording 26.5% in 2012, the highest in the world.[14]

In the last few years, Africa has recorded declining prevalence rates and resulting deaths. Southern Africa enjoys the highest uptake of antiretroviral treatment in Africa, as well as of prevention of mother to child infection transmission (PMTCT). In 2012, 68% of people living with HIV and AIDS in Africa could access treatment, countries in Southern Africa recording 78-95% uptake. Why then does the Region continue to experience such impacts from the disease? A few possible explanations: first, the roll out of treatment is most uneven. For example, Botswana has reached 95% coverage, South Africa 80%, while the Democratic Republic of Congo has reached 38% of eligible people only. In some countries up to 80% of eligible people have not received treatment. Moreover, the gender gap in access to therapy has been observed in many of the countries.[15] UNAIDS further reports that 75% adults in Africa had not achieved viral suppression in 2012. In 2006, UNICEF wrote: "In recent years, there has been a surge in leadership and resources for the fight against AIDS, with 8.3 billion available in 2005 alone for responding to the epidemic in low- and middle-income countries. The impact of the epidemic on children, however, has yet to receive the priority attention it deserves."[16] Indeed, in 2012 children received less than 25% of antiretroviral treatment given to adults. Moreover and in all cases, the poverty of most people has not facilitated improved diet for effective therapy outcomes

As the table above shows, in the 2012 Africa recorded the highest new infections and AIDS related deaths, creating more orphans of AIDS. But there is much hope in Africa because of the declining rates, the roll out of treatment, and the containment of MTCT. Led by Botswana and South Africa, each year more governments increase budget allocations to HIV and AIDS, although many of them remain dependent on external support, thus putting at risk uninterrupted supply of treatment drugs. But the numbers of orphans of AIDS especially in Eastern and Southern Africa are not declining. To the contrary, the high numbers of people living with HIV and AIDS, including adolescents, most of them not on treatment, signal a likely increase in the number of orphans in the next few years.

Challenged and weak health systems. The Council for the Development of Social Science Research in Africa took a historical perspective to analyze the weakening health systems in the

Region. After attainment of independence, many African governments invested heavily in public health systems: in structures, equipment, drugs and training of medical staff. Most of the public medical centers functioned relatively well , and many urban and some rural people could access medical care. From mid 1980s, however, many countries suffered economic crises, resulting in severe setbacks to the health sector from which many are yet to recover. Governments subjected the sector to severe budgetary cutbacks, and health institutions experienced sharp deterioration of the physical infrastructure and equipment base. Severe shortages of drugs and other necessary supplies became the norm. Alongside, and perhaps because of, this the sector witnessed a mass exodus of doctors and nurses to wealthy institutions in the West. To help the sector to remain functioning, governments introduced policies such as cost-sharing. As people got poorer, such policies, against the backdrop of weakened public health systems, "acted as a disincentive for continued popular access to and use of the services of the public health institutions."[17]

The crises spurred the emergence and/or expansion of private health systems. Private medical providers have grown in numbers and offer complex and quality services. International providers have joined this market; some local doctors have returned to their homes; while a number of newly qualified doctors have chosen to remain in their countries. Some of these moonlight their services to private providers. Others have set up private clinics or hospitals. They work in the public sector but also make time to service their private institutions. Alongside this has emerged and expanded the private health insurance market.

This state of health systems has led to three things: (i) majority poor, among them most of the orphans, have to do with the public health system such as it exists. Many, even in urban centers, do not see any doctors; they have to wait in long lines to see a nurse or medical orderly; and sometimes they do not get to be seen by any one. In rural areas long distances to health centers discourage many from accessing what available services there are. Many poor people self- diagnose and treat, or they seek alternative medical care from herbalists, traditional or faith healers. The downside of this is that, often, they wrongly self-diagnose and medicate themselves; some traditional or herbal 'doctors', whose numbers have surged, at pace with the weakening public health systems, are not sufficiently qualified in today's diseases. This author is not aware of any concerted study on faith healing, but word out there is that some of the healers see gaps in the public health system as a way to make money.

(ii) There has emerged in African countries a dual system of health service provisioning. The poor cannot afford private services. The small percentage of the rich and middle class Africans, who also make policies, utilize the private institutions. Take an example of South Africa, a country endowed with a rich medical infrastructure, including research and medical innovations, whose health care expenditure as percentage of GDP in 2007 was higher than that of the United Kingdom, yet it records one of the worst dual systems in health service provisioning in the world.[18] The inherited discriminatory system is yet to be sufficiently dismantled. Thus, to majority poor, good and accessible health services remain unattainable.

(iii) Unequal access to health services in much of Africa has contributed to the Region's high numbers of orphans. In addition to AIDS, other diseases and medical challenges have played a significant role in the creation of orphans. Of these, malaria and cervical cancer top the list. John Hopkins' Malaria Research Institute states that 10% of hospital admissions in Africa are due to malaria.[19] Globally, numbers of people who died of malaria in 2012, was put at 627,000 (down from 660,000 in 2010). 90% of these deaths occurred in Africa, 54% of them of children under 5 years.[20] But we do not have the actual numbers of orphans the disease has created.

Cervical cancer threatens the lives of many women. Inadequate early detection facilities have contributed much to this. For example, a woman in the United States of America has a 70% chance of surviving cervical cancer. In Africa, she has a 21% chance.[21] In 2008, World Health Organization (WHO) recorded 275,000 deaths globally. 50,000 deaths occurred in Africa. WHO further estimates that in Africa, 53,000 women die of the disease every year.[22] Challenges that public health services have faced against a backdrop of poverty make it almost impossible for majority women in Africa to access available resources for managing cervical cancer. As in the case of malaria, we do not have the exact figures of orphans this disease has created. But in the absence of armed and civil conflicts, after AIDS the two have contributed significantly to deaths of parents and creation of orphans.

Natural disasters: Natural disasters have hit almost every sub-region of Africa. The Sahel region has experienced persistent droughts, subjecting many citizens to untold suffering. The UN Food and Agricultural Organization have analyzed the effects of the changing climatic expressions over the last 50 years: the Sahel dryness has expanded; the West African region has experienced fluctuating weather patterns: in more recent past, 2009 brought irregular rains and drought conditions. These resulted in food shortages and intense malnutrition. 2010 experienced heavy rains, leading to improved food supplies in some areas, but generally resulting in serious floods. 1.8 M households were affected. Against a background of poor governance, trans-boundary animal diseases, socio-economic crises, the effects of natural disasters continue to dig deeper, including leading to death and affecting many families and children.[23] UNAIDS has blamed natural disasters as part drivers of the spread of HIV. These disasters have intensified poverty, forcing many young women and girls to prostitute themselves in order to provide for their families.[24]

Eastern and the Horn of Africa have not been spared. In 1998-2000, droughts hit Ethiopia and Eritrea, striking at a time of armed conflict between the two countries. Millions of dollars were diverted to the war effort, leaving citizens in both countries without much support. 100,000 deaths from starvation were recorded in Ethiopia. We do not have casualty figures for Eritrea, but we know that about 750,000 fled their homes. An unspecified number died from malnutrition and starvation. Together with Eastern Africa, the Horn was hit by the drought of 2010-2011. A total of 13 M people were reported affected, including 2M in Ethiopia, 850,000 in Kenya, and 455,000 in Somalia where 150,000 were children and mothers. Tens of thousands died. The UN declared the food crisis in Somalia as famine, the first in the 21st century.

Earlier in 2006, the East African sub-region had suffered another drought when 11 M were reported hit. In 2008-2009 yet another severe food crisis occurred because of irregular rains. Then, 10 M people were affected. Some children became orphans.[25]

Abject poverty: In itself poverty does not cause death, but it underlies and influences how people respond to some of the causes outlined above. Today, Africans are some of the poorest in the world, despite the Continent's many natural resources and minerals. Poverty has augmented many internal conflicts. Well off people, in influential positions, may engineer the conflicts, but many inhabitants join the struggle because of poverty. Some feel that they have nothing to lose since they are poor; others are led to believe that by supporting a conflict instigator, they might benefit once that person is in a leadership position. People have joined protests believing that their concerns, driven by poverty, might receive some attention. Instead, many end up losing their lives. AIDS has been linked with poverty precisely because poverty has pushed especially young women (and boys) into relationships that have exposed them to the virus. Some adolescent heads of families have picked up the disease in this way. Poverty has also affected the impact of antiretroviral treatment. Poor people are not able to follow the nutritious diet required for treatment's effectiveness.

Poverty and wealth have determined which side in the dual health system one ends up on. Poor people cannot afford tests for many of the diseases and thus they easily succumb to them. Cervical cancer that has not received much investment is a case in point. But perhaps a direct link with poverty is more easily and directly demonstrated by natural disasters. These affect access or non to food, death of parents, and orphanhood. When crops fail, better off people do not starve. It is always the poor who lack food and water, who die of starvation. It is poor people's children who become malnourished, their women and babies who suffer during pregnancy and breast feeding periods. Unless and until poverty is eliminated, or at best alleviated, orphans will remain challenged, whether they live with relatives or by themselves.

The Impact on orphans: Almost every African from Eastern, including Ethiopia, and Southern Africa has been touched by loss of a close family member: parent, brother, sister, niece, nephew, or close friend. The present author falls in this category. They share experiences, to learn from each other and to draw strength as they shoulder responsibility of the orphaned children. Some of them have formed organizations to assist many other orphans who may lack adequate support. Thus, they know from their contacts with family orphans and those they support some of what orphans go through after loss of parents. First is the emotional impact: to kids under age five, there is a sense of bewilderment as to why "mummy/daddy has been put in a hole"; after a while: "when will s/he come back from that place?" Later, because the parent does not come back: "does s/he not love me?" They fear loss of love. When old enough to understand death, they get angry: at the world; at those who are alive including their care givers; and at the deceased parent/s. In Africa, there are not sufficient counseling facilities. To many orphans these feelings remain for a long time, so that some develop death wishes.

At times, the community may not help. Often, neighbors conclude AIDS as cause of husband and wife deaths. They express these conclusions in many ways to the orphaned children, who may end up withdrawing into themselves. The stigma is more savagely and openly expressed by fellow children within the community and/or at school. Some orphans have stopped going to school because of this, while others may be transferred to a caregiver in a different part of the country for their protection. Yet, as they grow older, orphans treasure education, considering it a means to a better future. Consequently, often there is underlying fear of loss of school. Indeed, some orphans have been pulled out of school, either because of lack of funds by the hosting family or s/he would have to be taken to a rural area to live with a grandmother who lives miles away from a school. Thanks to the emergence of community schools, the ratio of orphan school attendance at elementary and primary levels has been rising, and actually reaching 100% in seven countries.

Some orphans have ended up with relatives who may have taken responsibility of other orphans. The family may be crowded in one room. But children can adjust rather quickly, if they are well loved and happy. A bad scenario is where the orphan is abused. Stories are told of especially girl children being treated as free labor and in some cases as sexual objects for males in the hosting family. Male orphans are not preferred because in most cultures girls and not boys help with household chores. Unloved, many boys have moved to the streets.[26] But some girls have run away, to join children of the streets.

Child-headed households: Perhaps the worst scenario is where children are left to fend for themselves. Cases have been witnessed where on the death of the surviving parent, relatives come to mourn and bury the dead person but also to take some property left by the deceased. It is possible that in such cases not much thought would have been given to the children, perhaps assuming that the State or some organization would come to their aid. Thus have risen households that are headed by children. The worst case the author has come across in Zambia involved a seven year old girl who had two younger siblings. None of the relatives checked what would happen to the children. After the funeral, they all left. Fortunately, a community organization had worked with the family during the parents' illness. Upon finding themselves in that situation, the seven year old went to the organization to seek help. Children have remained in the house; the organization has seen to their needs and provides protection.[27] Zambia Orphans Aid, USA, has assisted this family of youngsters over the last four years.

In Southern Africa, many such households are headed by girls. When boys become heads, as in the Democratic Republic of Congo, the tendency has been for them to work with girl-headed households so that the girl ends up as the *de facto* head of both households. In Uganda, there are more boys than girls with the responsibility of heading households.

Some scholars have argued that the numbers of such households are too few to warrant much concern within the broad spectrum of orphans. Our stand is that children as young as 7, 8, 11 years should not take on such responsibilities, even where there is an adult person from a local organization, church or government to check on them from time to time. Cases have been told of girls as young as 11 and 12 years in Eastern and Southern Africa who have been sexually exploited in order for them to raise money to buy a bag of corn meal or beans to feed their siblings. In some such situations, these heads have become pregnant, causing concern of their own safety from HIV and that of their babies. This author agrees with Charlotte Phillips who concludes that such households should not be seen as permanent. Any help to child-headed households should be short-term, governments indicating when the household would be phased out, by when alternative care arrangements would have been put in place.[28]

This critique is not to be interpreted that all orphans become miserable misfits. Some find the growing process very difficult; others receive love from family, foster parents, faith- based institutions and other care givers. With assistance in reaching their potential, they grow up into fulfilled and capable citizens. Nevertheless, orphanhood is a challenging condition that needs to receive serious and action-oriented consideration by both national and international communities.

Response: When impressionable orphan numbers showed up in the late 1980s and 90s, initial response came from within countries: from family members, including extended, community and non- governmental organizations, and orphanages. Close family members, or extended, responded, embracing their 'daughters', nieces and nephews. Within a few years, orphan numbers rose so sharply that in some situations one family could care for more than ten orphans. With many younger people dying, grandparents became and remain major providers of homes for the orphaned children, some inheriting up to 30 babies and children. If babies, grandmothers have had to dry- breast feed them, too poor to buy milk.[29]

In the early days, governments did not have programs to support these care givers. With time, family members, including grandmothers, have not been able to maintain the big families. As poverty levels rose, families started to live below the accepted poverty line. Care giving families have become overwhelmed. It has become very difficult for them to continue fulfilling the responsibility. What had been taken for granted, in African culture, has become a burden.

In a few societies, children have been fostered out to families not related to them. But in the early stages official monitoring had not been sufficiently developed, raising questions of their effectiveness. However, in some countries, such as Ghana, traditional care systems have stepped in. In rural Ghana, Queen Mothers train the care givers and monitor them.[30] Elsewhere, some communities have formed groups to assist orphan- hosting families, to undertake income generating activities to meet school requirements for the children and to provide food where needed. With the entry into this area of international organizations, community groups have turned themselves into community- based organizations, to apply for financial and technical assistance.

Alongside these, individuals, families, community based organizations and faith- based institutions built and ran orphanages. Some were built out of genuine concern for orphans. To some, however, orphan support became an industry. As middle class citizens with connections to the donor community and/or Africans in the Diaspora, they were able to raise money.

Because governments were slow in setting up policies to guide the care of orphans (and other vulnerable children), standards in some orphanages were not acceptable. Cases have been reported of registered orphanages that did not exist. Later, when governments set up systems for monitoring orphanages, some of such orphanages were shut down; others disappeared.

There has been much debate recently about the efficacy of orphanages. Some researchers see this care as something that should be transient, to keep the kids until their extended family members are identified. Some international institutions, including within the UN system, advocate this approach. They believe that the interests of the child are best served in a family environment; institutions are expensive per child; while staff turnover is high. This author is not versed enough in the research on this issue for a stand to be taken in this submission. But she has visited orphanages and children's villages in a number of African countries, in the context of her World Bank work on HIV and AIDS, and social protection. Yes, some of the orphanages are questionable. But probably more time needs to be allowed to examine different types of orphanages on one hand and the family situation and condition of children in the receiving homes on the other. Based on this, definitive conclusions may then be made. This would be a more realistic position because we know of some faith- based institutions that have been in existence for decades, deliberately organized to emulate family environments. We also need to understand social and economic pressures families are put to. Why do they take family orphans to churches; why do they leave babies on convent door steps; or at orphanage gates?

The international community has responded quickly on all fronts: to unaccompanied children in conflict situations, to provide emergency needs when natural disasters struck, in HIV and AIDS. The NGO *modus operandi* has been to identify local organizations to work with. They have brought financial and technical resources. Some Africans in the Diaspora have created organizations to mobilize financial support in the West, reaching orphans through community organizations and schools, and faith- based institutions. The AIDS field has received much attention in the last decade. PEPFAR is a case in point. Support through this mechanism has reached orphans through local organizations. The UN system has been active in supporting orphans, both at creating information to guide action and at mobilizing financial support. UNICEF, WHO and UNAIDS in particular have been very active at awareness raising within the system. Adoption also assists orphans. Inter country adoptions are slowly gaining recognition on the Continent, but to date this is in its infancy in Africa to make an big dent in the problem.

Conclusion: The main causes of the high numbers of African orphans seem poised to remain for some time. Yet, at this time, the millions of orphans whose needs are not met constitute a humanitarian imperative that will endure for at least a decade. The following offer opportunities at least for a minimum response:
- greater political will is needed at the national level to put in place result- based programs in support of orphans. Voices need to be heard on behalf of orphans
- funds should be established for orphans for their easier access to better health care
- higher education funds are needed for orphans, to include technical and entrepreneur skills training

- cash and in- kind support to child-headed families need to be intensified but for a specified timeframe, after which alternative care options must have been identified and offered to the children
- support to national and international organizations to develop tools for effective natural disaster preparedness
- support to be flexible enough to respond to shifting orphan care priorities.

Shimwaayi Muntemba, Dr./Ms.   June, 2014

References
Note: Africa, in this context, refers to Sub-Saharan Africa. Most of the documents cited hereunder may be found Online.
1. Global Church (2012): Surprising facts about orphans, Fact 1
2. UNAIDS (2013): Report on the global AIDS epidemic; UNICEF (2011):Childinfo; UNHCR (2012): Worldwide orphan statistics--SOS children's villages
3. UNAIDS (op. cit.)
4. Global Church (2012): Surprising facts about orphans, Fact 3
5. Pires, Richard-- in UNICEF, Eastern and Southern Africa (2014, May 2): South Sudan: Lost and alone: one girl's nightmare amid the violence
6. UN Office for Coordination of Humanitarian Affairs, South Sudan (2014, May)
7. Africa Heartwood Project (2014): Heartwood Orphan Home
8. Global Church (op.cit.)
9. Human Rights Watch (2003) "We'll kill you if you cry", sexual violence in Sierra Leone conflict; pers. comm. (2002-2004)
10. BBC documentary (2014): Women survivors of the genocide
11. International Crisis Group (2010, Nov. 18): Conflict risk alert, Guinea; Al Jazeera (2013, Aug. 8): Ethnic violence simmers in Guinea
12. Global Issues (2004): Nigeria and oil
13. UNAIDS (op.cit.)
14. Avert (2012): HIV & AIDS in Swaziland
15. WHO, UNICEF, UNAIDS (2013): Global update on HIV treatment: results, impacts and opportunities
16. UNICEF; UNAIDS; President's Emergency Plan for AIDS Relief (2006): Africa's orpharned and vulnerable generations: children affected by AIDS
17. Council for the Development of Social Science Research in Africa (2007): Private health provisioning in Africa
18. World Health Organization [WHO] (2010): Estimates for country health accounts
19. Johns Hopkins Malaria Research Institute (2014): About malaria
20. WHO (2013): World malaria report
21. WHO (2006): Controversial new vaccine to prevent cervical cancer
22. WHO, Regional Office for Africa (2012): Cervical cancer

23. Food and Agricultural Organization (2013): Disaster risk management strategy in West Africa and the Sahel
24. UNAIDS (2012): HIV prevalence in Sub-Saharan Africa
25. World Relief; Oxfam America (2014): Relief Web updates
26. USAID, (2002): Documentary on orphans in Zambia
27. Taonga Community Home-based Care, Kabwe, Zambia (2010)
28. Phillips, Charlotte (2011): Child- headed households
29. Sr. Philomena Schwegmann OP (2005): pers. comm.
30. Peters, Lisa (2008): Orphans and vulnerable children in Ghana

———————

Mr. SMITH. Ms. Jones, if would you proceed.

STATEMENT OF MRS. JOVANA JONES, ADOPTIVE MOTHER OF A CONGOLESE CHILD

Ms. JONES. Yes. Thank you for having me here.

We first saw our daughter, who we will name Ana Lei when she arrives, we first saw Ana Lei in April 2013 on a special-needs adoption Web site.

We decided early on to adopt an older child internationally with a hearing impairment because we read many cases where deaf older children are often overlooked and grow up without a language or the ability to communicate.

A few months ago, we were pleased to hear that Ana Lei's orphanage was within walking distance from a school, only to be disappointed that she was unable to attend and learn with the other children because of her hearing impairment. The idea of being trapped inside your own mind, frustrated with the inability to express your thoughts and feelings and ostracized from your friends—it is heartbreaking to even think about.

My family and I are the solution, if just for Ana Lei. We are willing, able, and ready to bring this princess into our home, to give her endless opportunities to love, communicate, share her dreams, fears, and excitement.

I love to educate myself in what would be her first language, American Sign Language. Over the last several years, I have taken courses and volunteered at Gallaudet, the deaf university just minutes from here. My family has participated in deaf events and attended deaf church services—anything we can do to immerse ourselves and increase our knowledge and skills in the deaf culture.

We also attend adoption conferences and take prep classes for adoptive parents so that we are fully aware of the good, bad, and ugly for when Ana Lei comes home.

Our children have been eagerly waiting, especially our biological daughter, for their sister to come home so they can have tea parties, show her dance moves, and sign bedtime stories. As a family, we enjoy signing during meal times, using captions whenever we watch TV, and having a weekly movie time where we watch an all-deaf, 30-minute educational kids show.

We homeschool our children, and we have Ana Lei's school desk and preschool supplies ready for her when she comes home. I have read books about teaching deaf children and have an awesome support group of moms homeschooling their deaf children.

My husband and we have been an Active Duty Air Force family for over 15 years. For the last 3 years, we have made it our mission to prepare financially and logistically for this adoption. We have sacrificed family vacations and held several fundraisers for this costly adoption. Our church was instrumental not only in giving but also in emotional and spiritual support.

Painstakingly but gratefully, we have raised all the funds needed for the adoption. We have bought furniture and prepped and painted Ana Lei's room. As a military-trained technician, my husband has planned to upgrade and install strobelight smoke detectors, doorbell signals, and other home devices for the hearing-impaired.

The nearby military bases will also offer family support through classes and workshops. And with the natural diversity that the military brings, our Congolese-American daughter will blend right into play groups, sport teams, and homeschool groups.

We are more than ready for Ana Lei's arrival. After years of studying, enduring financial burdens, not to mention the countless hours of reading, completing, and mailing reams of adoption forms, indeed, my family has sacrificed much. We realize, though, that our hardship is well worth Ana Lei's education, her happiness, and her life.

As adoptive parents, we have spent years preparing, and it is imperative that our children come home immediately. We have done our part. Our families have done all we can, and we are at our limit. We boldly ask for the backing and the support of our President, our Congressmen, and our elected officials, that you all draw your focus on removing any further delays of the adoption process within the countries of Africa.

We sincerely appreciate the efforts that have been made thus far, but, frankly, it is not enough. It is not enough until we have each orphan home with his or her American family. Each moment of delay makes it more difficult for them to adjust and more challenging for the parents to provide care.

Our arms are open now, and our homes are ready to receive them today. We pray that our Government mirrors our dedication and does its due diligence to bring our children home.

Thank you.

Mr. SMITH. Ms. Jones, thank you very much. I pray that also and hopefully we will all do our due diligence and accelerate our efforts on your behalf and all the others have that have been left behind, so thank you very much.

[The prepared statement of Ms. Jones follows:]

Jovana Jones
Adoptive Parent
16 July 2014 – The Growing Crisis of Africa's Orphans
House Committee on Foreign Affairs

We first saw our daughter, who we'll name Ana Lei when she arrives—we first saw Ana Lei in April 2013 on a special needs adoption website. We decided early on to adopt an older child internationally with a hearing impairment because we read many cases where deaf, older children are often overlooked and grow up without a language or the ability to communicate. A few months ago, we were pleased to hear that Ana Lei's orphanage was within walking distance from a school, only to be disappointed that she was unable to attend the school and learn with the other children because of her hearing impairment. The idea of being trapped inside your own mind, frustrated with the inability to express your thoughts and feelings, and ostracized from your friends—it's heartbreaking to even think about.

My family and I are the solution, if just for Ana Lei. We are willing, able, and ready to bring this princess into our home to give her endless opportunities to love, communicate, share her dreams, fears, and excitement.

I love to educate myself in what would be her first language– American Sign Language. Over the last several years, I've taken courses and have volunteered at Gallaudet, the deaf university just minutes from here. My family has participated in deaf events and attended deaf church services...anything we can do to immerse ourselves and increase our knowledge and skills in the deaf culture. We also attend adoption conferences and take prep classes for adoptive parents so that we are fully aware of the good, bad, and ugly for when Ana Lei comes home.

Our children have been eagerly waiting (especially our biological daughter) for their sister to come home so that they could have tea parties, show her dance moves, and sign bedtime stories. As a family we enjoy signing during meal times, using caption whenever we watch TV, and having a weekly movie time where we watch an all-deaf, 30-minute educational kids show. We homeschool our children and we have Ana Lei's school desk and preschool supplies ready for her when she comes home. I have read books about teaching deaf children and have an awesome support group of moms home schooling their deaf children.

My husband and we have been an Active Duty Air Force family for over 15 years. For the last 3 years, we've made it our mission to prepare financially and logistically for this adoption. We've sacrificed family vacations and have held several fundraisers for this costly adoption. Our church was instrumental, not only in giving, but also in emotional and spiritual support.

Painstakingly, but gratefully we've raised all the funds needed for the adoption. We've bought furniture, and prepped and painted Ana Lei's room. As a military trained technician, my husband has planned to upgrade and install strobe light smoke detectors, doorbell signals, and other home devices for the hearing impaired. The nearby military bases will also offer family support through classes and workshops, and with the natural diversity that the military brings, our Congolese American daughter would blend right into playgroups, sports teams, and homeschool groups.

We are more than ready for Ana Lei's arrival. After years of studying, enduring financial burdens, not to mention the countless hours of reading, completing, and mailing reams of adoption forms—indeed my family has sacrificed much. We realize, though, that our hardship however, is well worth Ana Lei's education, her happiness and her life.

As adoptive parents, we've spent years preparing and it is imperative that our children come home immediately. We have done our part. Our families have done all we can and we are at our limit. We boldly ask for the backing and support of our President, congressmen, and elected officials, that you all draw your focus on removing any further delays of the adoption process within the countries of Africa. We sincerely appreciate the efforts that have been made thus far, but frankly it's not enough. It's not enough until we have each orphan home with his or her American family. Each moment of delay makes it more difficult for them to adjust and more challenging for the parents to provide them care. Our arms are open now, and our homes are ready to receive them today. We pray that our government mirrors our dedication and acts now so that our children come home soon.

Mr. SMITH. Ms. Hunegnaw?

STATEMENT OF MS. MULUEMEBET CHEKOL HUNEGNAW, SENIOR DIRECTOR, MONITORING & EVALUATION AND KNOWLEDGE MANAGEMENT PROGRAM QUALITY AND IMPACT DEPARTMENT, INTERNATIONAL PROGRAMS, SAVE THE CHILDREN

Ms. HUNEGNAW. Thank you.

On behalf of the Save the Children, I thank you for the opportunity to testify today on this critical issue and request that my full statement be submitted for the record.

Save the Children is a nonprofit, child-focused organization working in the U.S. and in more than 120 countries and is considered a global leader in humanitarian and development assistance. We build capacity for countries to deliver and provide support for health, education, protection, and disaster relief services for more than 125 million children every year.

We are on the ground in countries across Africa, programming and advocating for those policies, programs, and funds that strengthen families and government systems to care for children. There are a range of factors that drive the vulnerability of orphans and children throughout Africa, including HIV/AIDS, maternal mortality, conflict and violence, and extreme poverty.

The term "orphan," consistent with PEPFAR's definition, is defined as a child who has lost one or both parents. In almost all cases, the other parent or close family members are alive and present in a child's life. Throughout Africa, kinship care is a powerful and important concept.

In this testimony, I will highlight and elaborate on four approaches that are key to an effective U.S. response to protect and support these children: First, strengthening families who are the frontline support systems for children; and, second, strengthening protection systems which can address the range of needs for families and communities; and, third, addressing the growing problem of children becoming the caretakers; and, lastly, continuing to develop better strategies for supporting children in families who are affected by conflict.

The crisis of Africa's orphans has been fueled over the last 15 years by HIV/AIDS, altering more than 20 million children's lives through loss of a parent or being infected themselves. In addition, their situation is compounded by threats associated with armed conflict and terrorism, including trafficking, sexual violence and exploitation, abduction, and recruitment into armed forces. With weak child-protection systems in many African countries, children are becoming more vulnerable, especially in countries affected by ongoing violence and conflict.

Orphans and vulnerable-children services include holistic care and support services per OVC guidance, including psychosocial care and support, household economic strengthening, social protection, child protection, education, and health and nutrition. Strengthening the systems that support vulnerable children and families ensure that children who are infected with HIV receive the support they need and that children who are affected do not become infected as they grow up.

One element of OVC programming that we are increasingly focused upon because of the success and importance is strengthening families. Looking at the child in the context of his or her family and community has shown to be the most effective approach and indicates the need to further integrate those programs that address the needs of children and their caregivers holistically, including maternal and child health, HIV/AIDS treatment, home-based care, economic resilience, and child protection. We understand the role that strong families, including extended families, play, ensuring that children can grow and develop healthy and reduce the risk of harm to children.

Another positive trend in orphans and vulnerable-children programming is an increased awareness and focus on the value of social protection to support Africa's orphaned and vulnerable children. Strong social welfare systems are critical to ensuring that investments to mitigate the impact of HIV/AIDS and poverty on Africa's orphaned and vulnerable children are sustained.

Our work builds the support for vulnerable children within their own communities, assisting them in getting protection, food security, economic strength, and access to basic health and education. We identify children who are orphaned and vulnerable and link them to an appropriate service that meets their needs.

A challenge but critical component of OVC programming is support for the needs of children as caregivers. Evidence shows that children in Africa, most of them become the dominant caregiver to family members when living with HIV/AIDS-infected parents who have chronic illness and may be approaching death, caring for increasingly frail grandparents, or leading households and caring for young siblings. The precise scale of child-caring remains unknown but is likely to be widespread and impacts many parts of their lives, including their ability to get an education.

Finally, one of the biggest challenges for OVC programming for an implementer is protecting and supporting children located in conflict-affected or fragile states. For these children, the already difficult circumstances and complexity of needs is compounded with the fragility, uncertainty, and unsafe environment.

In these areas, Save the Children has seen a rise in sex trafficking, street children, and children being placed in institutions. This presents a significant child-protection concern, as these children are often without the guidance of an adult caregiver, and the situation is compounded by increased exposure to threats associated with armed conflict. With child-protection systems weak or completely destroyed due to conflict, protecting orphans living in fragile states is complex.

Looking forward, Save the Children would welcome the subcommittee's support to address the plight of orphans and vulnerable children in Africa, and we would like to highlight two areas where congressional involvement would have a powerful impact on children's lives.

First, Save the Children is a strong supporter of USAID's 2012 OVC guidelines and their comprehensive approach to care, including child protection, education, health care, and early childhood development and family strengthening. We are profoundly appreciative and supportive of the funds that Congress included as a requirement that programs for orphans and vulnerable children continue to be 10 percent of all PEPFAR program funds. Any dilution or reduction of those funds or commingling of those funds with those for treatment should be discouraged, and it would threaten our ability to provide this essential service for children.

Second, we strongly support the codification of the whole-government Action Plan for Children in Adversity. The action plan and its primary three objectives—strong beginnings, protective family care, and reduction of violence against children—are all goals that I hope we can share. Codifying these priorities through legislation would support a more comprehensive approach, encourage efficiencies and coordination across government agencies, shared outcomes, and accountability.

In conclusion, we thank the subcommittee for its continued leadership on U.S.-African global issues and would like to continue to be a resource for you in the future. We ask for your continued partnership with us to invest in children so that they have what every child deserves: The right to not just survive but thrive.

Thank you.

[Ms. Hunegnaw's prepared statement was submitted after the hearing and appears in the appendix.]

Mr. SMITH. Thank you so very much, Ms. Hunegnaw. Let me ask you a question with regards to—does your organization consider adoption a form of protection?

And I say that because there is a huge gulf between people who view adoption, inter-country adoption especially, as a form of human trafficking, which I find absolutely unconscionable.

And I can give you an example. When Romania ended its inter-country adoptions—I mentioned earlier that I had worked on human rights vis-à-vis Romania from my very first days in the U.S. Congress in 1981. And when Nicolae Ceausescu lost his reign of terror as the President of that country, unelected, huge numbers of orphanages were discovered where kids were literally abandoned. And adoption flourished, on and off, but it did flourish, and there were a large number of inter-country adoptions.

A woman by the name of Lady Nicholson, who was the rapporteur for the EU in terms of ascension into the EU from Romania, made it very clear that a prerequisite for ascension into the European Union was an end to inter-country adoption. And she construed all inter-country adoptions as a form of human trafficking.

And I would note parenthetically, as the author of the Trafficking Victims Protection Act of 2000, the landmark law to combat human trafficking at home and abroad, I take a backseat to no one in my absolute abhorrence of human trafficking. And that is why The Hague Convention was formulated as a way of facilitating it's end.

But I am just wondering if your organization does look at adoption as a form of protection for children.

Ms. HUNEGNAW. Thank you.

Save the Children supports enabling families to care for children. We believe unnecessary separation of children from their families should be prevented.

Mr. SMITH. Yes.

Ms. HUNEGNAW. We promote appropriate and permanent family care for children. But we believe that inter-country adoption should be an option only when it follows the standards and regulations contained within The Hague Convention.

Our primary focus is making sure that children are cared for in a family context, as much as possible in their country of origin, and inter-country adoption is taking up only as an option when that is not available.

Mr. SMITH. Mr. Stockman wanted to comment, and then——

Mr. STOCKMAN. Yeah——

Mr. SMITH [continuing]. Ms. Dempsey, I think you might want to——

Mr. STOCKMAN. Yeah, go ahead.

Mr. SMITH. Or——

Mr. STOCKMAN. Well, I have, actually, a question for Ms. Dempsey.

Ms. DEMPSEY. Yes?

Mr. STOCKMAN. And I get to ask this because it is asked of me, quite frankly, often, because we shipped medical supplies to DRC. In fact, one of the most dangerous trips I think I ever took was from Brazzaville to Kinshasa on that little boat.

And I am wondering, what motivated you to get involved in this? And how often do you go to Africa? And how do you describe your personal experience?

Ms. DEMPSEY. I come to this work as an adoptive mom. And overcoming the obstacles I encountered in my own Government to bring my daughter home from Vietnam is the reason I do this work. I came, realizing that there was a deficit in advocacy for families, and I shifted my practice, frankly. And it has become my life's work to help bring orphaned children into families when they need it.

The DRC crisis started in September, and at Both Ends Burning we were monitoring it. And when it became obvious to us that the Department of State wasn't meaningfully engaged—and the way that it became obvious to us was that they couldn't even tell us how many people were impacted, how many children were impacted, how many sick kids were at risk, they couldn't give us basic information—we decided that we needed to step in and help the families become organized and advocates for themselves.

So my interest is in helping these families. I come to this work from a very personal commitment to kids, but it has become my life's work.

I haven't actually traveled to Africa. I hope to do that very soon. So most of our efforts have been focused on engaging Members of Congress and the administration to help Department of State find its way to make this an urgent humanitarian crisis and find a solution to it.

Mr. SMITH. If my friend would yield?

Mr. STOCKMAN. Yes, I will.

Mr. SMITH. We have with us today Whitney Reitz from the USCIS, who actually did the investigation of Ethiopia when those allegations were made. She led the interagency delegation to Addis Ababa in early 2011. She reviewed many cases on site at the Embassy and then analyzed a database of over 4,000 cases.

And her team's finding was 75 percent of the cases were clean and nonproblematic, 25 percent had problems generally of a clerical nature, and just 5 percent presented factors that would warrant a closer investigation, which, clearly, indicated a far better record than the holdups and for the lack of responsiveness would indicate and, of course, I would say on behalf of our subcommittee, we are very grateful for the work that you did on that, Ms. Reitz.

But you say, Ms. Dempsey, in your testimony, again, getting back to Kinshasa, that when the numbers exploded—"explosive" was the word you used—from a handful to several hundred of adoptions in the DRC, that their inability to handle the casework led to mandatory field investigations for all cases.

Were there other proximate causes? Were they genuinely concerned about other mitigating factors that might say there is a problem here? Or was it just a matter of this slows the process?

Ms. DEMPSEY. Well, I wish they were here to answer that question. I——

Mr. SMITH. Well, you know, before you answer it, we did invite the Office of Children's Issues to be here. And we have turned this hearing into part one of a two-part hearing process. We will invite Ambassador Susan Jacobs to be here. She has testified before my subcommittee on previous occasions, particularly as a relates to child abduction.

And I would note parenthetically, I have a bill that is pending in the Senate right now that passed on December 11th in the House which the Department seemingly was against—Secretary Kerry changed that position, and now they are for it—on child abduction, another hat that the Office of Children's Issues handles.

And it was all from what I learned in dealing with the case of David Goldman, whose child was abducted to Brazil. Five years later and a whole lot of mistakes later, he finally got his son back. So it incorporates all the lessons learned there.

And I think we need to be moving even more aggressively forward on this issue of child abduction, as well, so that we can get this right. So if you could maybe speak to that.

You also testified that there was a lack of resourcing. And if you have any idea of how many resources need to be deployed here. And any of you might want to speak to that.

And you also brought up the issue of where the central authority should be housed. And that was a big issue in the year 2000 faced by Congress; do we go to HHS, or do we go to Department of State? I am not sure that should be revisited, maybe it should, but if you could speak to that, as well.

Ms. DEMPSEY. Well, those are a lot of questions, and I will try to do my best to answer them. Please let me know where I fail, because I certainly will.

With respect to the Department of State's motives in implementing the 100-percent mandatory field investigations, it is my understanding that they deemed the growth itself to be problematic, and nothing more than that.

And that is a tried-and-true tactic that we have seen from the Department of State. Any time a program experiences growth, what you and I would regard as a success for children is deemed a problem at the Department of State Office of Children's Issues and in the U.S. Embassies. And they start to view every case with suspicion and mistrust and looking for bad actors and bad actions.

And while we certainly want them to make sure that these cases are ethical, transparent, well-done, that the kids are legitimately orphans in need of permanent families—we expect that of them— what we know is that they don't use the right tools to do that. And, instead, what they are doing is slowing down a system and engaging with foreign governments and adoptive families in a way that is, frankly, offensive and ineffective.

So I look forward to the second round of this, and I look forward to their questions on that specific issue.

With respect to the Office of Children's Issues as our central authority, what I can say based on the numbers and my personal and professional experience with them is that they are failing children. They are failing children in need, and they are not advocating for permanent solutions for children.

Part of that is that their mandate is too narrow, I believe. They are tasked with enforcing Hague, promoting Hague, and that becomes an inherent conflict of interest in non-Hague countries. And our Hague expectations are perhaps unrealistic in developing nations, who simply lack the infrastructure and resources to integrate all that is necessary to become a partner under Hague.

And so what I would suggest is that we engage them in collaboration and we help them build systems that work and serve children well, instead of pointing fingers and making accusations and allegations that are unsubstantiated. And that is what we are doing today.

So I believe Children in Families First, the pending bill, does a very good job of addressing the solution. It removes the Office of Children's Issues from primary responsibility for child protection and child welfare, and it would create a new office to do that. Both Ends Burning fully supports it. We are a member of the working group, and we would like to see that legislation move forward as quickly as possible.

I don't think that is the solution for the DRC kids today. I think that will take too long, and we can't make the fundamental change that is necessary. And so what we are looking for from Congress on the DRC crisis is immediate intervention at the highest levels and reaching out to DRC in the way that the Department of State has failed to do.

Mr. SMITH. Would anyone else like to address that?

And in the case of Kinshasa, was there, in your opinion, Ms. Jones perhaps, how long before they informed you of the tardiness of this process?

And you mentioned, Ms. Dempsey, the Department of State could and should have been actively involved from the moment the suspension went into effect to find a solution. When did they get involved?

Ms. DEMPSEY. Well, they announced it 2 days after it went into effect. So they issued an alert. It wasn't until June that they asked families with sick kids to come forward and to provide medical records and to identify themselves. That is 9 months after the adoption crisis began. That is 10 children who perished in the meantime. And that was only after Congress called on them to make that happen. It wasn't until May that they could provide any-body, in Congress or otherwise, with the number of families who were involved in this crisis.

And so they claim to have been actively engaged from the start. I would suggest the results tell us otherwise. It wasn't until Congress issued a mandate and sent a letter to President Kabila that we saw the few kids that have come home come home.

And while we celebrate every victory and we are so grateful for the 21 children who have come home, there are hundreds more waiting, and we can't rest on that and consider ourselves vic-torious. We have a lot of work to do.

Mr. SMITH. Did you want to respond, Ms. Muntemba?

Ms. MUNTEMBA. Yeah, Mr. Chair. I think I want to—I am very interested in this subject, but I want to underline that for Africa, really, adoption is very, very much a new thing, and it is in its in-fancy.

And in terms of addressing the problem of orphans as it is now, we can obviously bring that in, but there are so many more issues that we are struggling with at the moment, that people are trying to deal with. For example, what she says there. There is so much push on let families look after their kids, not adoption, not orphan-ages, not this and that, and yet we are not helping these families. So I would like to know, what are we doing to strengthen this?

What I know and my research has shown me, the extended-fam-ily system is really breaking down in Africa. So if we want these kids to be with families, to be in the family environment, we have to strengthen them. What are we going to do about that?

Because adoption, unless you really, really push it, it is very— I mean, I adopted my sister's son, and it wasn't easy for me. As an, in my culture, I would say mother, older mother, it wasn't easy for me to bring him here. So, I mean, it is not a solution that we can see in that next 10, 20, 30 years.

But the breaking down of family systems is where I think we have to push for your help at the moment. What can you do to push African governments to help at that level?

Mr. SMITH. None of us ever said that adoption was the only solu-tion; it is just part of a comprehensive approach.

I will never forget, 10 years ago, a decade ago, Greg Simpkins, who is our staff director on this subcommittee, and I were in Addis Ababa and went to an AIDS orphanage, and we had five kids on each arm as we walked through the place. Big smiles. Just kids looking for a place to go. And we know that some of those kids were not adoptable because it was an economic and—you know, the extended family could not care for these AIDS orphans.

But it underscored to me—and this is an experience I will never forgot—the desperate need for affection and love and a stable home where they could grow up in.

And the people who ran it were obviously absolutely committed. It was faith-based. It was backed by USAID. But, you know, there was only so much they could do.

But it is just part of the solution. None of us are ever saying this is a panacea. But your point is well-taken.

Mr.——

Mr. STOCKMAN. Yeah.

Ms. Jones, can I ask a question? Two things. You mentioned you would take her to church. And are you from here locally, and which church is it?

Ms. JONES. No. My children—we have never met our adopted child.

Mr. STOCKMAN. And which country?

Ms. JONES. So she is from DRC, so she is from Congo, so we have never met her before. But we are just preparing to have her here, so we do attend different services, you know, that have deaf children and deaf services.

Mr. STOCKMAN. Yeah, I have a deaf staffer on staff. But I am wondering, when I was over there—and I guess, have you been—you obviously——

Ms. JONES. We have never been.

Mr. STOCKMAN. Okay. Well, I was wondering—I am actually going to ask the committee on this—have any of you been to DRC? Because the problem there is just more than—there are a lot of problems there. It is very problematic in so many ways. It is the size of Western Europe; it is a very large country. And in the eastern half, there is guerilla warfare, on and off for many years, so many people have been killed there. And the government seems to be thriving on bribes. When you leave, they ask for money. So it is inherently a challenging country, not just for adoptions but even for travel.

And I am wondering if you could tell the committee or us what you think we could do to facilitate more pressure on the government. Because I understand that the President actually will be here in about 2 weeks, so I will bring this topic up with him. But I also think he is probably meeting with the chairman.

Are you meeting with the—yeah, well, he is coming here in 2 weeks. Yeah.

So I guess my question to you is, what message would you like us to carry to the President?

Ms. JONES. I would like to say that, you know, that we—you know, there are a lot of criteria that the adoptive parents have to go through. And we are going through each one, even if there are new things that are brought to us after we have finished, you know, 6 pages and 30 pages of, you know, different forms. You know, so we are doing all that we have to do.

And so we just want to, I guess, have things—you know, get things in writing, you know, to say, okay, well, these parents have done this. You know, there should be no reason why these kids are waiting. So we need explanation on why we are waiting.

I think one thing that we have to do, we have to pay for when the children come home. Our agencies have to come out and do post-adoption and make sure that the kids are happy and we are taking care of them and we are doing what we said we were doing. And so then I asked our agency, I said, well, if we have to do these things and we are paying for this service, why is it a question to the other country? And then she says to me, well, they never see the post-adoptions; that is only for the agency.

So if there is any way that we can or the President can make sure that all the post-adoptions that we are paying for, all the pictures and the questions that are being asked, if we are taking care of them, if they are happy, if they are thriving, you know, can those countries, can DRC, can they have that information? Is there any way that they can have that information so that is not a question so that is one less thing that we have to worry about?

Mr. SMITH. Let me, if I could, Ms. Dempsey, you made a point that adoptions have declined 69 percent over the last 9 years and that the Department of State has simply continued in its primary role as gatekeeper instead of building a base of child welfare and child protection expertise.

We know that Russia obviously cut off adoptions in 2012, so included in that figure would be—you know, we still had countries of origin that were willing to provide a means of adopting children. That number, you know, a cynical take on that would be that there might be a bias against adoption. What is your take on that? Is it a lack of——

Ms. DEMPSEY [continuing]. Being cynical.

Mr. SMITH [continuing]. Foreign Service Officers having too many cases?

On the child abduction case, parenthetically, and in a parallel fashion, in hearings that I held here with the Office of Children's Issues, a big question I would often ask is, what do you do with the files? What kind of action, advocacy do you take to make sure things actually happen, particularly when there are obstacles strewn in the path of an adopting parent or, in that case, an abducted child and a left-behind parent? What do you do to really navigate that and make sure the country is facilitating it with their government authority so that, you know, children are protected but, you know, these delays, interminable delays, are overcome?

Ms. DEMPSEY. We have seen a tremendous decline in the number of adoptions. Part of that is attributable to the sending countries' unilateral decisions, as we saw in Russia. China has a concentrated effort to reduce the number of adoptions, and it was a large sending country.

But we have also seen programs close for reasons that I have already discussed. Similar to what we see in Ethiopia and what we see in DRC, Nepal closed in 2010, and that was a decision made by the Department of State and USCIS. Absent a statutory mandate to do so, they suspended the processing of adoptions, closing the door to hundreds, if not thousands, of orphaned children based on suspicion.

I will tell you that that program closed under allegations that all the children were trafficked. All 56 cases in the pipeline at that time were investigated, and not a single one of them had been trafficked. Every single one of them was a legitimate orphan, and every single one of them now lives here in the United States. We are now approaching the fourth anniversary of the closure of that program, and it remains closed, inexplicably.

And so I would say that there is a bias against international adoption in the Department of State and that child welfare and child permanency is not on the dance card of the Office of Children's Issues. Instead, they are focused on processing cases and doing so in a way that slows the process for families and children.

Mr. SMITH. Anything else?

Yes, ma'am?

Ms. HUNEGNAW. Thank you. I just wanted to answer. We are gathered here to talk about the Africa orphan crisis. It is a crisis because millions of children are in this state now—and I do personally agree, sincerely appreciate that inter-country adoption may be one option to address this issue.

But in terms of looking at the magnitude of this crisis, Save the Children believes in looking at a systemic approach to this, focusing on families, and especially in Africa, where kinship care is the system and the custom. What we focus on is what is in the best interest of the child and how we prepare these families, who are already overstretched, from meager resources to care for an additional child, an additional family member in their families.

So I would like to just highlight again those two focus areas that I have made in my earlier comment that resources—Congressman, you mentioned about what kind of resources are needed. I think protecting the commitment is very much important. We do appreciate the commitment that is already made, but protecting that commitment and increasing those resources to help us support those families to protect the children is very important, and also looking at the holistic needs of those children, because of the magnitude that we have in Africa today.

Mr. SMITH. Thank you.

Ms. Jones, if I could ask you—first of all, thank you for your service to the Air Force and to this country. As you point out, 15 years, you are an Air Force family.

You point out that, ''My family and I are the solution, if just for Ana Lei. We are willing, able, and ready to bring this princess into our home to give her endless opportunities to love, communicate, share her dreams, fears, and excitement.'' And you talk about the hearing impairment and how, you know, you want to make the difference in her life to really help her with that.

Has that impairment grown worse? If you could elaborate on that. Because delay is often denial, and even though she is not as young as some others who are adopted, when it comes to a medical or any other condition, delay can mean further impairment that does not get turned around.

So if you could just speak to that issue, and anyone else who would like to touch that—again, the idea that if the care is not being provided and your home is ready, willing, and able to provide it, that seems to be a huge setback for the child.

Ms. JONES. Yes. As I mentioned, you know, she is deaf. And the orphanage there has a school within walking distance, and these children are learning English and they are learning basic skills just so that they can have some type of skill. And so, for her, she doesn't have that option.

We don't get updates of how great she is doing. The only time we get an update is when we get invoiced when she is sick with malaria or she has a toothache that needs to be paid for. So those are the only updates that we get.

Our agency let us know, when we bring our home, she will be on the developmental level of an 18-month-old. Even though she is 5 on paper, we believe she is about 7, but there is—I want to say there is no hope for her. She understands how to walk, talk, and use—I mean, walk, use the bathroom, and gesture of what she wants but cannot fully communicate.

We send picture books over, and we have pictures of her looking at our family book and videos, but she has no clue. When she waves—she repeats what she sees. And she would wave the whole video until someone takes her hand and put it down. And she just has this look of, "I don't know what is going on," you know?

So she needs to be home so that she can begin to express herself and let us know what her needs, her wants are. And she is just not getting that there.

Mr. SMITH. Yes?

Ms. DEMPSEY. I would just like to add, with respect to the children who are ill and life-altering conditions, life-threatening conditions, the DGM recently announced last week that they would not consider the medically fragile cases anymore. And the Department of State's response to these families was, too bad, you just need to sit and wait until the suspension is lifted.

And I would expect more urgency from them. On behalf of these children, on behalf of these families, I would expect them to say, we are going to be doing everything in our power to change or reverse this decision so that more children don't die.

I know I don't need to remind you, but I want to say again for the record that children are dying during this wait. Children who have families here ready to provide for them are perishing needlessly. And we need our Government to act with a sense of urgency.

Mr. SMITH. Your point has been very well-taken.

And you said you have knowledge of at least 10——

Ms. DEMPSEY. Yes.

Mr. SMITH [continuing]. Who have passed away, for whom that would have not have been the case?

Ms. DEMPSEY. Yes, sir.

Mr. STOCKMAN. I would just thank you for coming out. I appreciate it. And it has opened my eyes. But anybody that has worked with the DRC on any level, including humanitarian aid, it is a challenge. And I think the chairman and I will be dedicated to making sure that this hopefully will be resolved. Thank you.

Mr. SMITH. Yeah.

Just one question, Ms. Dempsey, you might be able to answer. What part of the Department of State addresses international child welfare and protection?

Ms. DEMPSEY. I am not aware of any part of the Department of State that addresses child welfare and child protection, which I think is a fundamental flaw.

Mr. STOCKMAN. Who is the—you said you talked to Department of State. Do you want to tell us after the hearing who that was, or——

Ms. DEMPSEY. I will tell you in the hearing.

Mr. STOCKMAN. Okay.

Ms. DEMPSEY. I am talking to the Office of Children's Issues. The primary communications are coming from the desk——

Mr. STOCKMAN. Okay.

Ms. DEMPSEY. She is simply the messenger.

Mr. STOCKMAN. Yeah.

Ms. DEMPSEY. But it is coming from the Office of Children's Issues and the Embassy in Kinshasa.

Mr. STOCKMAN. The Embassy. Okay. Thank you.

Mr. SMITH. Anything you would like to add before we conclude the hearing? And, perhaps, in that, if you would like to, if Susan Jacobs was sitting here rather than down at her office, what would you say? And, again, we will convey your testimonies to them in the spirit of encouragement and part-admonishment, but if there is anything you would like to say before we close?

Ms. DEMPSEY. I would just like to thank you sincerely for the opportunity to appear today and to share this information with you all and for all that you have done already for the children in need and all that you are committing to do going forward. The crisis can't be solved today, but it needs to be solved, and we need to be working toward that.

With respect to Ambassador Jacobs, I welcome the opportunity to sit with her and to discuss these issues with her and to help the Department of State do their job better. I have been rebuffed in my personal——

Mr. SMITH. Did you say rebuffed?

Ms. DEMPSEY. Yes, when I have offered to share my learnings and findings.

And so I would ask—what I would like to know from the Department of State is why they are doing 100-percent field investigations, in what number of cases are they finding fraud—my guess is it is a very small number—what amount of resources they need to be more effective in doing their job, and why they are not advocating with a sense of urgency on behalf of these families.

Thank you.

Mr. SMITH. Thank you.

Ladies?

Ms. HUNEGNAW. I also want to thank you for this opportunity. And I would like to say that Save the Children would be happy to be a partner with the subcommittee or your staff to help them work on this issue. Thank you for the opportunity.

Mr. SMITH. Thank you.

Ms. JONES. And I would like to thank you, too, for the opportunity to be the voice not only for my child but for the other adoptive moms and dads and parents out there that are ready to bring their children home.

Mr. SMITH. Ms. Muntemba?

Ms. MUNTEMBA. Thank you for the opportunity. And I look forward to continuing discussions and broaden help for African orphans, of AIDS especially, and for children in conflict areas.

And, one of these days, I would like to really say, how are you going to help us beyond adoption? Because, really, the need is great out there.

Mr. SMITH. No, I hear you.

Ms. MUNTEMBA. And maybe, as Congresspeople, you can help push for that help to come from the U.S., the USAID and national country offices, and maybe we can get more help that way.

Thank you.

Mr. SMITH. That point is well-taken.

And the larger scope of the hearing today, again, we would have loved to have had the Office of Children's Issues here, and we will make that request again. But Nancy Lindborg, who is a very competent and very effective person with whom I personally and this subcommittee in toto have had a very good working relationship with, she is very committed, as is her staff, on that larger issue that you mentioned, which is why I opened up with the first 1,000 days of life as being absolutely transformative for the next 30,000 days of that child into adulthood, individual person.

And if it doesn't start in the womb, the susceptibility to malaria and a host of other diseases is greater, the immune system is far less efficacious in fighting off diseases than if you start while he or she is still an unborn child. And that needs to grow exponentially in Africa, in Latin America, elsewhere, Asia, and this country as well.

So I would like to thank—Steve, if you have any further comments? Or are we——

Mr. STOCKMAN. No.

We just have a great chairman, that is all. It is unanimous.

Mr. SMITH. Well, we will follow this up with a part two, and we will invite Ambassador Jacobs, or her designee, but I do hope she will come, especially to hear, you know, testimonies the likes of which we heard today. But we will give her your testimonies, as well.

So thank you.

And the hearing is adjourned.

[Whereupon, at 5:10 p.m., the subcommittee was adjourned.]

A P P E N D I X

MATERIAL SUBMITTED FOR THE RECORD

SUBCOMMITTEE HEARING NOTICE
COMMITTEE ON FOREIGN AFFAIRS
U.S. HOUSE OF REPRESENTATIVES
WASHINGTON, DC 20515-6128

Subcommittee on Africa, Global Health, Global Human Rights, and International Organizations
Christopher H. Smith (R-NJ), Chairman

July 15, 2014

TO: MEMBERS OF THE COMMITTEE ON FOREIGN AFFAIRS

You are respectfully requested to attend an OPEN hearing of the Committee on Foreign Affairs, to be held by the Subcommittee on Africa, Global Health, Global Human Rights, and International Organizations in Room 2172 of the Rayburn House Office Building (and available live on the Committee website at www.foreignaffairs.house.gov):

DATE: Wednesday, July 16, 2014

TIME: 2:00 p.m.

SUBJECT: The Growing Crisis of Africa's Orphans

WITNESSES: Panel I
The Honorable Robert P. Jackson
Principal Deputy Assistant Secretary
Bureau of African Affairs
U.S. Department of State

The Honorable Nancy Lindborg
Assistant Administrator
Bureau for Democracy, Conflict and Humanitarian Assistance
U.S. Agency for International Development

Panel II
Ms. Kelly Dempsey
General Counsel and Director of Advocacy and Outreach
Both Ends Burning

Shimwaayi Muntemba, Ph.D.
Founder
Zambia Orphans of AIDS

Mrs. Jovana Jones
Adoptive mother of a Congolese child

Ms. Muluemebet Chekol Hunegnaw
Senior Director
Monitoring & Evaluation and Knowledge Management Program Quality and Impact
Department
International Programs
Save the Children

By Direction of the Chairman

COMMITTEE ON FOREIGN AFFAIRS

MINUTES OF SUBCOMMITTEE ON _Africa, Global Health, Global Human Rights, and International Organizations_ HEARING

Day _Wednesday_ Date _July 16, 2014_ Room _2172 Rayburn HOB_

Starting Time _2:00 p.m._ Ending Time _5:09 p.m._

Recesses | 1 | (_2:37_ to _4:03_) (___ to ___) (___ to ___) (___ to ___) (___ to ___) (___ to ___)

Presiding Member(s)

Rep. Chris Smith

Check all of the following that apply:

Open Session ☑   Electronically Recorded (taped) ☑
Executive (closed) Session ☐   Stenographic Record ☑
Televised ☑

TITLE OF HEARING:

The Growing Crisis of Africa's Orphans

SUBCOMMITTEE MEMBERS PRESENT:

Rep. Karen Bass, Rep. Ami Bera, Rep. Steve Stockman

NON-SUBCOMMITTEE MEMBERS PRESENT: _(Mark with an * if they are not members of full committee.)_

HEARING WITNESSES: Same as meeting notice attached? Yes ☑ No ☐
(If "no", please list below and include title, agency, department, or organization.)

STATEMENTS FOR THE RECORD: _(List any statements submitted for the record.)_

Statement for the record from Ms. Muluemebet Chekol Hunegnaw of Save the Children, submitted by Ms. Muluemebet Chekol Hunegnaw
Both Ends Burning report, submitted for the record by Ms. Kelly Dempsey
Statement for the record from Catholic Relief Services, submitted by Rep. Chris Smith
Statement for the record from World Vision US, submitted by Rep. Chris Smith
Statement for the record from Christian Alliance for Orphans, submitted by Rep. Chris Smith

TIME SCHEDULED TO RECONVENE _____
or
TIME ADJOURNED _5:09 p.m._

Gregory B. Simpkins
Subcommittee Staff Director

Muluemebet Chekol Hunegnaw

Senior Director, Monitoring & Evaluation and Knowledge Management

Program Quality and Impact Department, International Programs

Save the Children

HOUSE COMMITTEE ON FOREIGN AFFAIRS

Subcommittee on Africa, Global Health, Global Human Rights, and International Organizations

July 16, 2014

The Growing Crisis of Africa's Orphans

On behalf of Save the Children, I thank you for the opportunity to testify before the Subcommittee today on an important and critical issue. I would request that my full statement be submitted for the record.

Save the Children is a nonprofit, child-focused organization working in the US and in more than 120 countries and is considered a global leader in humanitarian and development assistance, serving as a preeminent voice for children with governments, civil society and private sector partners for over 80 years. We build capacity for countries to deliver and provide direct support for health, education, protection, and disaster relief services for more than 125 million children. As a program implementer and advocacy organization, we have a unique perspective: we are on the ground in many countries across Africa, programming and advocating for those policies, programs, and funds that strengthen families and government systems to care for children and leverage success. As such, we would like to share with you some of the successes and challenges in orphans and vulnerable children (OVC) programming in Africa, as well as some of the key contributions that the U.S. government can make moving forward.

There are a range of factors that drive the vulnerability of orphans and children facing adversity throughout Africa, including HIV/AIDS, maternal mortality, conflict and violence and extreme poverty. The term "orphans and vulnerable children", are defined as a children who have lost one or both parents, and children who are vulnerable due to HIV/AIDS, inadequate adult support, life outside of family care, marginalization or discrimination.[1] In almost all cases, a parent or close family members are alive and present in a child's life. As such, the first priority of interventions to assist these vulnerable children is to strengthen their family. Throughout Africa, kinship care is a powerful and important concept and we need to do more to understand it and to strengthen caregivers, but also to ensure that it provides a protective and safe environment for all children.

Within this definition and context of orphaned and vulnerable children, this testimony will highlight and elaborate on four points that are key to an effective U.S. response to protect and support these children:

- We must continue to invest in strengthening families, who are the frontline support system for children;
- We must continue to strengthen social protection systems which can address the range of needs for families and communities;
- We must do more to prevent children from becoming primary caregivers to their families; and
- We must continue to develop better strategies for supporting children and families who are affected by conflict.

As background, the crisis of Africa's orphans has been fueled over the last 15 years by HIV and AIDS. HIV/AIDS has irreversibly altered the lives of over 17 million children who have lost one or both parents to the disease, as well as the lives of over 3.4 million children who themselves are infected with the HIV and face an endangered childhood and uncertain future.[2] The AIDS epidemic has deepened poverty in many communities, as the burden of caring for the vast majority of orphans and vulnerable children falls on already overstretched extended families; women or grandparents with the most meagre resources. New insight also shows children as young as 8 becoming primary caregivers.[3] Such households are expected to earn 31% less than other households.[4] Without a real safety net, street

[1] Orphans and Other Vulnerable Children Guidance for United States Government In-Country Staff and Implementing Partners. PEPFAR 2006. Available from: http://www.pepfar.gov/documents/organization/83298.pdf

[2] PEPFAR Guidance for Orphans and Vulnerable Children Programming. PEPFAR. July 2012. Available from: http://www.pepfar.gov/documents/organization/195702.pdf

[3] *Child Carers*. Save the Children 2010 Available from: http://www.savethechildren.org.uk/resources/online-library/child-carers-child-led-research-with-children-who-are-carers

[4] Aids Orphans in Sub Saharan Africa. Available from: http://www.un.org/events/tenstories/06/story.asp?storyID=400

life is the recourse for many orphans, who often suffer from poor health, trauma and psychological distress, making them more vulnerable to abuse and exploitation.[5]

In addition to HIV and AIDS, the situation of Africa's orphaned and vulnerable children is compounded by threats associated with armed conflict, terrorism (Nigeria) including trafficking, sexual violence and exploitation, abduction, psychosocial distress, family separation and recruitment into armed forces. With child protection systems weak or non-existent in many African countries, children are becoming more vulnerable. This is especially the case in countries afflicted by ongoing violence, war and other conflict.[6]

OVC services include comprehensive, holistic care and support services per the OVC guidance including: psychosocial care and support, household economic strengthening, social protection, child protection, legal protection, education, health and nutrition and child welfare systems strengthening. Strengthening the systems that support vulnerable children and families ensure that children who are infected with HIV receive the support they need and that children who are affected don't become infected as they grow up. It's not only the right thing to do; comprehensive OVC programs also contribute to effective prevention and utilization of HIV treatment and other health services. These systems also make sure that children do not continue to face other harms to their growth and development and that their families, the first line of defense for these children, are adequately supported to care for these children over the long term. Strengthening the families will help decrease the need for institutionalization, reduce the numbers of children living on the street, and help ensure that children are able to reach their full developmental potential.[7]

Save the Children is a leader in the global response for orphans and children affected by AIDS and other adversities including conflict. We play a major role in new developments in the field, including focusing attention on the age and developmental stages of children, needs of caregivers, investments in strengthening government social welfare systems, and community systems for the care and protection of children who are without appropriate care.

One element of OVC programming that we are increasingly focused upon because of its success and importance is strengthening families.

---

[5] *Recensement des enfants de la rue de la ville province de Kinshasa*, UNICEF, 2006, as cited in "Project Appraisal Document" *op. cit.*, p. 35.

[6] For example: The 2011 "Document de la stratégie de croissance et de réduction de la pauvreté (Seconde génération) " IMF. Available from: http://www.imf.org/external/french/pubs/ft/scr/2013/cr13226f.pdf

[7] PEPFAR Guidance for Orphans and Vulnerable Children Programming. PEPFAR. July 2012.

The Importance of Strengthening Families

Looking at the child in the context of his or her family and community has shown to be the most effective approach and indicates the need to further integrate those programs that address the needs of children and their caregivers holistically including maternal and child health, HIV/AIDS treatment, home-based care, and child protection.[8] There is a strong emphasis on the caregiver with a focus on ensuring that the mental health needs of the caregiver are addressed and parenting skills are enhanced to build families' resilience in providing a nurturing (emotionally and cognitively), protective environment for children to grow into healthy, productive adults.[9] We also support approaches that build the economic resilience of the households to be able to adequately care for their children. We understand the role that strong families play in ensuring that children can grow and develop healthily and reduce risk of harm to children. In the case where children lose their primary caregivers, extended families need support to assume responsibility for these children and provide a safe and protective environment for these children to grow.

Children who have lost one or both parents, or who are infected or affected by AIDS, conflict or other adversities are at a distinct disadvantage, especially with regards to education, nutrition, health, safety, and development. They require access to quality education and health care services. They also require stable and protective caregivers.[10] As a result, programs that address only the clinical needs of these children miss out on a key opportunity to improve children's wellbeing far into the future.

Because the HIV pandemic puts great strains on the existing community-based safety net responses, it is essential we build family resilience through approaches that boost the household's ability to recover from shocks (e.g. illness, loss of income, etc) and improve their ability to cope even in the event of shocks and support -- and thereby strengthen the first line of response to build a safe and nurturing home environment.[11] Save the Children has been developing approaches that reach the most vulnerable young children who are at a distinct disadvantage. Our research on young children impacted by HIV and AIDS has revealed that early intervention is imperative and that children who are orphaned need critical and often long-term support to reach their developmental potential. We continue to support national

---

[8] Bell, B (2009) *A 'Rough Guide' to Child Protection Systems*, Save the Children

[9] Inequality in early childhood: risk and protective factors for early child development. Lancet, 2011

[10] Toxic stress: The facts. Center for the Developing Child, Harvard University.

[11] *'Strengthening National Child Protection Systems in Emergencies through Communty-based Mechanisms: A Discussion session.'* Save the Children UK and CPWG. 2010

governments to enhance their policies in support of this most vulnerable target group while working with communities and families to reinforce existing support systems.[12]

Another positive trend in OVC programming is an increased awareness and focus on the value of **social protection to supports Africa's orphaned and vulnerable children.**

Building Social Protection Supports

Strong social welfare systems are critical to ensuring that investments to mitigate the impact of HIV and AIDS and poverty on Africa's orphaned and vulnerable children are sustained over the long term.

Our work builds support for vulnerable children within their own communities, assisting them get protection, psychosocial support, food security, economic strength, and access to basic health and education services. Save the Children works across government and other civil society organizations to identify children who are orphaned or vulnerable and links them to appropriate services to meet their needs. A strong element of the program is our effort to boost household income through innovative savings and lending strategies that boost resiliency. These strategies allow caregivers to start small businesses which may earn sufficient income to meet basic needs.

Another challenge, but critical component to OVC programming, **is the awareness and inclusion of support for the needs of caregivers.**

Addressing the Needs of Children as Caregivers

Evidence shows that children in Africa most often become the dominant caregiver to family members when: living with HIV-infected parents who have chronic and debilitating illness and may be approaching death; living with and caring for increasingly frail grandparents who may have formerly been caring for the child; or leading households and caring for younger siblings, usually as older children or young adults.[13]

The precise scale of 'child-caring' remains unknown, but is likely to be widespread and unevenly distributed. Children are more likely to be caring in regions where HIV rates have been high for several

---

[12] The Essential Package. Availabel from: http://www.care.org/sites/default/files/documents/The_Essential_Package_Holistically_Addressing_the_Needs_of_Young_Vulnerable_Children_and_Their_Caregivers_Affected_by_HIV_and_AIDS_1_0.pdf

[13] *Child Carers.* Save the Children 2010 Available from: http://www.savethechildren.org.uk/resources/online-library/child-carers-child-led-research-with-children-who-are-carers

years and are continuing to climb, local sources of income are few (prompting healthy adults and children to migrate for work), proportions of single-headed households are high, health and social services are minimal (including Anti-Retroviral- Therapy access), and communities are, by default or design, relied upon to provide 'home-based care' to sick members. Children are also likely to assume caring responsibilities when a household is in severe economic decline and has little or no human capital with which to engage reciprocally in social networks. Social isolation puts immense strain on the child–adult relationship, and poses a risk to livelihood because food and other basic goods are not shared.

Data suggests that children as young as eight years take on the care of sick adults and siblings, and that these roles can continue for several years, perhaps for a series of sick or frail adults. Too little is known about the psychological impacts of emotional care and the assumption of responsibility, or 'parentification', by young children in African contexts. Older children, whose caring roles undermine their school attainment, recognize this long-term cost to their well-being. Child caregivers may manage to stay in school, but their attainment suffers owing to sporadic attendance, exhaustion and failure to complete tasks. Policies that focus only on improving enrollment among orphans and vulnerable children will not address this problem.[14]

Girls appear to have primary care responsibilities for siblings or sick/frail adults more frequently than boys. But gender divisions of labor are highly sensitive to socio-cultural preferences.

Close scrutiny of research investigating care dynamics within families and neighborhoods reveals that children are performing a physically, mentally and emotionally demanding set of tasks during a period in which their own lives are undergoing profound change. The experiences and implications of living with a parent or other close relative with acute, debilitating illness, as well as those of bereavement and grief, need to be better and more consistently integrated into our analysis of 'care'.

Protecting Children in Conflict-Affected and Fragile States

Certainly, one of the biggest **challenges for OVC programming for any implementer is achieving desired impact for children located in a conflict-affected or fragile State.**

For OVC living in conflict-affected fragile states in Sub Saharan Africa, the already difficult circumstances and complexity of needs is compounded with the fragility, uncertainty, and unsafe

---

[14] *Child Carers.* Save the Children 2010 Available from: http://www.savethechildren.org.uk/resources/online-library/child-carers-child-led-research-with-children-who-are-carers

environment. In these areas, Save the Children has seen a rise in sex trafficking, street children and children being placed in institutions. These issues present significant child protection concerns as these children are often without the guidance of adult caregivers. The situation is compounded in a fragile state context by the increased exposure to threats associated with armed conflict, including trafficking, sexual violence and exploitation, abduction, psychosocial distress, family separation and recruitment into armed forces. With child protection systems weak or completely destructed due to conflict, a response to protect OVC living in fragile states is complex.[15]

Save the Children is currently responding to the needs of OVC in Nigeria, Ivory Coast and the Democratic Republic of Congo (DRC). In these programs, we support approaches to strengthen families while mitigating the socioeconomic impact of AIDS which is often linked to extreme poverty. Our programs reinforce family structures, support community efforts to care for children and for children to stay with family members rather be placed in institutional care. Our program in the DRC serves approximately more than 7,000 children, including orphans made vulnerable by HIV/AIDS and other difficult circumstances and children who are currently living in dangerous environments, such as children living on the streets and engaged in hazardous labor, children illegally detained, and children who are being sexually exploited.

The Way Forward: Doing More to Protect Vulnerable Children

Looking forward, Save the Children would welcome the Subcommittee's support to address the plight of orphans and vulnerable in Africa, help meet their needs and ease their burden, and identify how our response can be improved collectively. Toward that end, we would like to highlight two actions that Congress could take that would have a powerful impact on children's lives:

1) Save the Children supports robust funding for PEPFAR and urges Congress to protect the 10 percent of funds dedicated to OVC. Save the Children is a strong supporter of USAID's 2012 OVC guidelines and their comprehensive approach to care including child protection, education, health care and early childhood development and family strengthening. We are also profoundly appreciative and supportive of the funds that Congress included as a requirement that programs for orphans and vulnerable children continue to be 10 percent of all PEPFAR program funds. Those funds are critical to

[15] Unlocking Progress in Fragile States – Save the Children UK
http://www.savethechildren.org.uk/sites/default/files/docs/Unlocking_Progress_in_Fragile_States_low_res_1.pdf

the provision of life-saving and life-changing services to some of the most vulnerable children on the African continent – those orphaned or affected by HIV/AIDS. Any dilution or reduction of those funds, or co-mingling of those funds with those for treatment should be discouraged as it would threaten our ability to provide these essential services for children.

2) We strongly support the codification of the whole of government *Action Plan for Children in Adversity*. The *Action Plan* and its primary three objectives: Strong Beginnings, Protective Family Care, and Reduction of Violence Against Children are all goals that I hope we can share. Codifying these priorities through legislation would support a more comprehensive approach, encourage efficiencies and coordination across government agencies, shared outcomes, and accountability. This plan furthers our interest in ensuring that US government investments for children in adversity, including orphans and vulnerable children, are strategically planned and implemented so that all children in adversity, living in all regions of the world, have access to programs and services that enable them to grow and succeed. In conclusion, we thank the Subcommittee for its continued leadership on U.S. Africa and global health issues and would like to continue to be a resource for you in the future. Save the Children is deeply appreciative of your efforts that are essential for giving children at home and around the world a fair chance in life. We ask for your continued partnership with us to invest in children so they have what every child deserves – the right to not just survive, but thrive.

MATERIAL SUBMITTED FOR THE RECORD BY MS. KELLY DEMPSEY, GENERAL COUNSEL
AND DIRECTOR OF ADVOCACY AND OUTREACH, BOTH ENDS BURNING

BOTH ENDS BURNING
PAPER CHAINS

Report on U.S. Government Actions and the Impact of these Actions
on Nepal's Abandoned Children, 2010-present

**Written by Kelly Tillotson Dempsey
and co-authored by Chad Turner, Morgan Abbott,
Cassandra Capote, Brett Currier, Kat Gardzalla, Erica Kassman, and Alyse Young**

Paper Chains

Both Ends Burning's Report on the U.S. Government's suspension of adoptions from Nepal details the misguided policies and actions of the United States Department of State and the United States Citizen and Immigration Services (USCIS). This Report centers on the suspension of adoptions from Nepal in August 2010 and details the devastating effect that the Government's actions had on American families and vulnerable children who were directly impacted. It makes clear that the actions of the Department of State and USCIS need to be reviewed and changed so that American families seeking to adopt children in need, where ever they may reside, do not suffer the same harm as that caused in this case. Absent immediate and substantial change to U.S. Government policies in regards to international adoption, the Department of State and USCIS will simply continue unchecked in deciding when to suspend adoptions from a country, resulting in immeasurable harm to homeless children and the American families seeking to adopt them.

I.   BACKGROUND

In 2007, international adoptions from Nepal were halted by Nepal in order to amend its adoption laws in an attempt to address allegations of widespread corruption and malfeasance then existing in the system. International adoptions from Nepal resumed in January 2009, after this two-year self-imposed closure of the program by Nepal.   In August 2008, after the closure of international adoptions in 2007 and prior to the resumption of adoptions in 2009, UNICEF issued a comprehensive study on international adoption in Nepal[1]. In this report, UNICEF found the new Nepali adoptions laws to be insufficient to address the issues that led to the 2007 closure of the program and inadequate to achieve compliance with the Hague Convention on Intercountry Adoption.

---

[1]http://www.unicef.org/nepal/ADOPTING_the_Rights_of_the_Child_UNICEF_Terre_des_hommes_Emba rgoed_29Aug08.pdf

Despite the concerns outlined in the 2008 UNICEF report, in early 2009, international adoptions reopened in Nepal. Dozens of American adoptions service providers became licensed to conduct international adoptions in Nepal. By the end of 2009, hundreds of American families had submitted their dossiers to Nepal and were registered with the Nepali Ministry of Women, Children and Social Welfare, waiting to receive referrals for children and enter the court process to finalize their adoptions. By this point, these American families had each invested a substantial amount of money, time and energy in their adoption, and believed they would be permitted to proceed with the support of the U.S. Government.

II. ACTIONS BY THE U.S. DEPARTMENT OF STATE

In February 2010, the Office of Children's Issues at the United States Department of State first signaled its intent to end international adoptions from Nepal[2]. The Department of State advised adoption service providers that their accreditation status would be put at risk if they continued to operate in Nepal and advised families wishing to adopt from Nepal that they should seek to adopt children from other countries. The stated rationale was "grave concerns about the reliability of Nepal's adoption system and the accuracy of the information in children's official files," based on a 2009 report from the Hague Conference's Permanent Bureau to Nepal[3]. The Department also stated:

> *Based on our own observations and experience with adoption cases in Nepal, the U.S. Department of State shares many of the concerns outlined in the Hague report. In one of the first cases processed by the Government of Nepal after the revision of the Terms and Conditions,* **the U.S. Embassy in Kathmandu found that the adopted child was not a true orphan** *and that his [SIC] birth parents were actively searching for her.*[4]

However, contrary to the assertion in the quote above, the U.S. Embassy played absolutely no role in discovering or righting this wrong. By their own admission, in a U.S. Embassy cable to D.C. in October 2009, the U.S. Embassy described the facts as follows:

---

[2]http://adoption.state.gov/country_information/country_specific_alerts_notices.php?alert_notice_type=notices&alert_notice_file=nepal_1

[3] http://www.hcch.net/upload/wop/nepal_rpt09.pdf

[4] Nepal Adoption Notice, *supra* note 2.

> *Post processed the first four files of American adopting families... Inquiries into all four cases resulted in inconclusive evidence of any wrongdoing and the GON [Government of Nepal] designated orphan status of the children was confirmed by Post.* **In one of the cases however, the American family withdrew their I-600A petition,** *citing what they felt were irregularities in on the part of the local police and the orphanage in addition to the child's behavioral problems.*[5]

In fact, the case of the withdrawn petition serves as an example of the Nepali system working as it was intended to function. Upon discovering that the child was not in fact an orphan and had two living parents the Nepali Government appropriately reunited the child with her parents[6]. Further, at the time of this Department of State Notice, it must be noted that **only four** U.S. families had filed adoption petitions with the U.S. Embassy in Kathmandu – an insufficient sample from which to draw any reliable conclusions based on its "own observation and experiences with adoption cases in Nepal."

A few months went by, and the Embassy continued to hear of more American families entering the pipeline of families wishing to adopt from Nepal – up to 300 new families according to reports from the Nepali government[7]. The Embassy's Consular Section of two employees feared an avalanche of work and reported their concerns to the Department of State headquarters, noting that they could not possibly conduct proper investigations of so many cases with such a small staff[8]. By this time, the Embassy had processed about thirty cases under the new legal system, **all of which were investigated and approved,** demonstrating the absence of any evidence of fraud.

---

[5] Cable from American Embassy Kathmandu to Secretary of State, *Nepal Intercountry Adoptions Resume: Concerns Remain*, October 2009.

[6] http://archives.myrepublica.com/portal/index.php?action=news_details&news_id=15599

[7] April 2010 cable from U.S. Embassy to D.C. re: "We cannot meet the demand for the market" says GON Adoption Official

[8] Id. ("We will conduct orphan investigations to the extent our resources will allow... However we are not confident that this effort will turn up many tangible leads...Post welcomes suggestions as to how it can conduct deeper field investigations with its limited resources."); see also February 2010 cable from U.S. Embassy to D.C. re; Widespread Corruption indicated in Intercountry Adoption System ("Post believes that its own internal investigations into the orphan status of the child may fruitlessly drain resources and may not provide sufficient evidence to prove that the child is not an orphan.")

Then in an unexpected turn of events, in August 2010[9], the Department of State and USCIS announced their suspension of new adoption petitions for children who had been abandoned in Nepal[10]. This announcement abruptly eliminated any chance for international adoption to serve as a viable option for abandoned or deserted Nepali orphans, and the vast majority of orphans in Nepal were abandoned or deserted. Hundreds of American families who had submitted their dossiers to adopt from Nepal were affected. Families awaiting referrals had their dreams of adopting from Nepal abruptly ended. Sixty-two American families with referrals of Nepali orphan children (the "Pipeline Families") were also adversely impacted, although the Department of State and USCIS agreed to continue processing these cases, albeit with strongly worded warnings about delays and concerns about their legitimacy.

Additional difficulties immediately followed this announcement, when the Department of State, through the Consular Section at the U.S. Embassy in Kathmandu, undertook the required "orphan investigations"[11] for each of the 62 cases then pending for the Pipeline Families. The orphan investigations began from the premise that the documents of abandonment for each child, including police reports and orphanage records, were inherently unreliable. The U.S. Embassy sought to corroborate the contents of the police and orphanage records through interviews of police officers, orphanage staff, and community members. In the end, the U.S. Embassy found absolutely nothing – no evidence of fraud. In 82 days, the U.S. Embassy completed all 62 investigations and had absolutely

---

[9] http://www.state.gov/r/pa/prs/ps/2010/08/145767.htm

[10] The Office of Children's Issues, the U.S. Embassy in Kathmandu and USCIS continuously refer to the children as abandoned. However, their use of the term "abandoned" is inaccurate as a matter of U.S. law. More precisely, these children were deserted. Indeed, according to the Foreign Affairs Manual, primary evidence of abandonment is a document signed by the parent(s) unconditionally releasing the child to an orphanage. 9 FAM 42.21 N13.2-5(3)(a). The children at issue are all foundlings, with no identifiable birth parents, and thusly are deserted children as defined by 8 CFR § 204.3(b).

[11] The orphan investigation is intended to verify the eligibility of the child to immigrate as an orphan to the United States under U.S. law. Department of State consular staff based at the U.S. Embassy act as USCIS' proxy for orphan adoption cases in countries, such as Nepal, where USCIS does not have its own physical presence. The Embassy consular staff has delegated authority to approve cases, but they do not have authority to deny them.

nothing to show for it. The U.S. Embassy touted the speed with which these investigations were "completed" as an impressive accomplishment, and the Chief Consular Officer was proud of the fact that each case had been investigated in little more than one business day.

At the close of the U.S. Embassy's whirlwind investigations, the Embassy approved six cases. However, for the remaining 56 Pipeline Families, the Embassy officers found the cases "not clearly approvable" and forwarded them to the USCIS Field Office in New Delhi for review. Given the allegations made by the Department of State and the Embassy's refusal to approve 90% of the Pipeline Families' cases, the adoptive families and their adoption service providers braced for more bad news. USCIS approved one of the cases and issued "Requests for Evidence" to each of the 55 remaining families (the "Pipeline Cases"), citing the U.S. Embassy's concerns about indicators of fraud in the Nepali adoption system and requiring the families to provide additional information about the circumstances of the child's abandonment or to find the birth family.

III. ACTIONS TAKEN BY AMERICAN ADOPTIVE FAMILIES

The law is undeniably clear that orphan classification is not appropriate for cases involving "clear and documented evidence of child-buying, fraud or misrepresentation"[12]. However, in all of the Pipeline Cases there existed absolutely no evidence at all—clear and documented or otherwise—of fraud, child-buying, or misrepresentation. One need not even review the cases to confirm this fact – The Chief U.S. Consular Officer in Nepal confirmed the absence of any evidence of fraud on a conference call with the Pipeline Families in December 2010[13]. The U.S. Embassy's failure and refusal to approve the I-600 Petitions (Petition to Classify Orphan as an Immediate Relative) filed by the Pipeline Families, especially in light of its admission that there was no evidence of fraud, was an abdication of its duty to the

---

[12] *See* 9 FAM 42.21 N13.2-8(a).

[13] *See* Nepal Adoption Series Conference Call #3, 986_1618 (Mr. Bird and Ms. Benavidez affirming that there were no indications of fraud).

American families it serves, and their adopted children, not to mention the thousands of Nepali orphans denied the opportunity to be adopted as a result of the closure of Nepal.

Despite the obstacles, the Pipeline Families were determined to proceed, so they hired lawyers, traveled to Nepal, and paid investigators to go over the same ground that the Department of State had already travelled in investigating these cases. They did so, but far more thoroughly and competently than the Department of State. **In every case, without exception or condition, USCIS ultimately approved the Pipeline Cases. No fraud was found and the Pipeline Families were finally able to bring their children home to the United States.** However, the Pipeline families also discovered, in every case, without exception or condition, that the Department of State's orphan investigation had been poorly conducted and improperly documented.

Although the Pipeline Families and their adopted children were eventually united, additional damage had been done to each child as the result of unnecessary months spent languishing in orphanages, where, day by day their health and mental development was further impaired. **The waiting children needlessly spent, on average, an additional 201 days in institutions. In addition to the emotional damage done to the Pipeline families during this period, they also had to incur in excess of $25,000, on average, to address the unsubstantiated allegations made by the Department of State.** American families felt that they had to fight their own government to protect their adopted children, at great personal expense and extraordinary emotional cost.

IV. ACTION NEEDED

As bad as the experience was for these children and their families, **far greater damage has resulted to the children who are still languishing in Nepal's orphanages today.** The suspension has denied these abandoned and deserted orphan children the opportunity to find permanent loving families and also denied American families the opportunity to provide loving homes for these children.

The actions of the Department of State were unnecessary, and predicated on suspicions rather than fact.

An objective analysis of the facts, detailed in full in the Both Ends Burning Report, leads one inexorably to the conclusion that the Department of State decided without any substantial evidence to support its decision, to end international adoptions from Nepal. Based on the facts presented in this report and the evidence provided to USCIS by the Pipeline Families that no fraud was occurring, the Department of State and USCIS should have re-evaluated their policy, lifted the suspension, and allowed adoptions from Nepal to resume. But the U.S. Government has steadfastly refused to re-open Nepal for adoption, clinging still to its unsubstantiated allegations of widespread fraud[14].

Both Ends Burning believes the facts show that American adoptions from Nepal should never have been suspended and at minimum should be reopened to American families since no fraud has been demonstrated. Both Ends Burning asks Congress to review the actions taken by the Department of State and USCIS in suspending adoptions from Nepal and to pursue the lifting of the adoption suspension. The abandoned and deserted children of Nepal deserve to have the chance of being raised by a family and there are hundreds of American families willing to welcome them with open arms. An arbitrary decision by two U.S. Government agencies, not based on substantial and documented evidence, should not permanently destine homeless children to life without a family to love and care for them. .

---

[14]http://adoption.state.gov/country_information/country_specific_alerts_notices.php?alert_notice_typ e=notices&alert_notice_file=nepal_5

MATERIAL SUBMITTED FOR THE RECORD BY THE HONORABLE CHRISTOPHER H. SMITH, A REPRESENTATIVE IN CONGRESS FROM THE STATE OF NEW JERSEY, AND CHAIRMAN, SUBCOMMITTEE ON AFRICA, GLOBAL HEALTH, GLOBAL HUMAN RIGHTS, AND INTERNATIONAL ORGANIZATIONS

Statement of Michele Broemmelsiek
Vice President, Overseas Operations
Catholic Relief Services

To the House Committee on Foreign Affairs
Subcommittee on Africa, Global Health, Global Human Rights, and International Organizations

Hearing: *The Growing Crisis of Africa's Orphans*
July 16, 2014

Thank you, Chairman Smith, for convening this hearing and allowing civil society and the faith-based community to share its experience supporting orphans and other vulnerable children (OVC). We are grateful that Congress took action last fall to extend the President's Emergency Plan for AIDS Relief (PEPFAR), and we were particularly pleased with the continuation of the 10% OVC set aside. This is one of the largest and most important sources of dedicated funding for programs that support children affected by HIV. In fact, these funds have improved the health and well-being of more than 5 million vulnerable children as of FY2013.[1]

Globally, there are more than 150 million children who have lost one or both of their parents due to a variety of causes such as accidental death, disease, and conflict. Of these, roughly 17.8 million have lost a parent due to HIV-related illnesses; most reside in sub-Saharan Africa.[2]

However, studies show that nearly 90% of children designated as 'orphans' by international agencies actually have a surviving parent[3,4] and approximately 95% of all children directly affected by HIV, including those who have lost parents, continue to live with their extended family.[5] But when a child loses a parent to AIDS, that child is three times more likely to die – even when that child is HIV negative.[6] These children often live in households that are under extreme emotional and economic duress, and may suffer from any number of hardships that impede their ability to thrive; malnutrition, limited access to education and health services, exposure to stigma, discrimination and exclusion. Children in households affected by HIV/AIDS must often step up and prematurely assume the role of caretaker and breadwinner. Research continues to show the devastating differential impact of HIV on children; for example, children affected by AIDS have increased risk of mental health problems, exposure to physical, emotional and sexual abuse, school drop-out,[7] stunting[8] and death.[9]

Maintaining children within a family structure, but supporting them through community-based programs that provide nutritional support, economic strengthening, vocational and educational training, health care, and psychosocial support are essential to protecting children at risk. Therefore, the OVC service that Catholic Relief Services promote strengthen households so that vulnerable children have the opportunity to live in a family setting, attend school, enjoy better nutrition, and maintain social and emotional attachments. Moreover, CRS works with families and children to bolster their livelihood options, thereby increasing the sustainability of these

---

[1] Office of the Global AIDS Coordinator (OGAC). 2014. PEPFAR Annual Report, 10th Annual Report to Congress. Washington, D.C.

[2] United Nations Children's Fund (UNICEF). 2014. *The State of the World's Children*.

[3] Belsey, M. 2008. The family as the locus of actions to protect and support children affected by or vulnerable to the effects of HIV/AIDS: A conundrum at many levels. Learning Group 1: Strengthening Families. Harvard University, Cambridge, MA: The Joint Learning Initiative on Children and AIDS; 2008.

[4] Sherr, L. et al. 2008. A systematic review on the meaning of the concept "AIDS orphan": Confusion over definitions and implications for care. AIDS Care, 20:527–536

[5] Hosegood, V. 2008. Demographic evidence of family and household changes in response to the effects of HIV/ AIDS in southern Africa: Implications for efforts to strengthen families. Learning Group 1: Strengthening Families. Harvard University, Cambridge, MA: The Joint Learning Initiative on Children and AIDS.

[6] Mermin, J. et al. 2005. Cotrimoxazole prophylaxis by HIV-infected person in Uganda reduces morbidity and mortality among HIV-uninfected family members. AIDS, 19: 1035-1042.

[7] Cluver, L. 2011. *Children of the AIDS pandemic*. Nature, 474:27-29.

[8] Ndirangu, M. et al. 2011. *Nutritional status of under-five children in HIV-affected households in western Kenya*. Food and Nutrition Bulletin, 32(2):159-67.

[9] Newell, M.L. et al. 2004. *Mortality of infected and uninfected infants born to HIV-infected mothers in Africa: a pooled analysis*. The Lancet, 364, 9441, 2004:1236-1243.

interventions. These holistic services not only protect the physical health of children, but offer them the greatest chance of thriving in supportive family setting.

As part of our OVC service strategy, CRS works with national governments and their health and social systems, as well as with communities, to strengthen families through access to essential support services. OVC services also play a critical role in HIV prevention, particularly among adolescent girls. Recent research has demonstrated the influential role OVC services have in reducing HIV risk behavior among adolescents.[10,11,12,13] When children are infected by HIV, OVC support services and other socio-economic interventions are essential to increasing pediatric treatment and ensuring that children have the necessary support to remain on treatment and access critical health services. However, despite the powerful role that these services can have upon HIV affected families, currently, only 11% of highly vulnerable children[14] and their households access essential support services.[15]

We firmly support efforts to increase pediatric treatment, but we urge you to preserve PEPFAR's 10% set aside for OVC services and avoid co-mingling those funds with PEPFAR's much larger resources designated for treatment. The original intent of the set aside was to mitigate the devastating impact of HIV on children and adolescents living in affected households. While expanded pediatric treatment is essential, our concern is that the much needed funding for traditional OVC programming will become diluted (due to the disproportionately higher costs for pediatric treatment), resulting in an effective reduction of the 10% set aside. This would significantly reduce vital services for children that reduce child mortality, morbidity and vulnerability.

We make this recommendation based on our significant experience supporting adults and children living with and affected by HIV. Last year, CRS-supported programs provided HIV-related treatment, care and support for more than 1.3 million people in 30 countries across Africa and the hardest-hit regions of Asia and Latin America. The total value of these programs was more than $51 million.

Over the last decade CRS has been one of PEPFAR's largest implementing partners. Among our most significant programs has been AIDSRelief, our PEPFAR-supported antiretroviral treatment (ART) program. CRS was prime grantee for this project, which provided HIV care and treatment for more than 700,000 people in ten countries, including more than 22,000 children who remain enrolled on lifesaving ART. In addition, our PEPFAR OVC project served 179,000 children in six countries from 2004 to 2010. In addition, more than 17,000 caregivers received services such as training on child protection, psychosocial needs of children and economic strengthening for the whole family.

These achievements were made possible through the deep commitment of the Office of the Global AIDS Coordinator (OGAC), the U.S. Congress and the President to combat HIV. Together, we have made a difference in the lives of many of the world's most vulnerable people, especially children.

PEPFAR and other US supported programs serve as a lifeline for people living with and affected by HIV and improve HIV prevention and treatment outcomes among children, youth, and adults. As strong proponents of OVC programs, we at CRS strongly urge the safeguarding of the 10% OVC earmark as separate from pediatric funding (in accordance with US Congressional intent and mandate) and increasing pediatric treatment investment under PEPFAR's already robust 50% treatment funding set aside.

Thank you for your time and continued support of orphans and vulnerable children in Africa.

[10] Cluver, L., et al. 2013. *Child-focused state cash transfers and adolescent risk of HIV infection in Aouth Africa: a propensity-score-matched case-control study.* The Lancet Global health, 1:e362-70.

[11] Cluver, L., et al. Inpress. *Cash plus care: social protection cumulatively mitigates HIV-risk behavior among adolescents in South Africa.* AIDS (IAS Special Issue). Expected publication date: July 2014.

[12] Hallfors, D., et al. 2011. *Supporting adolescent orphan girls to stay in school as HIV risk prevention: evidence from a RCT in Zimbabwe.* American Journal of Public Health, 101(6): 1082-8.

[13] Cho, H., et al. 2011. *Keeping adolescent orphans in school to prevent HIV Infection: evidence from a RCT in Zambia.* Journal of Adolescent Health 48(5):523-

[14] Current coverage data is drawn from programming that serves children infected or affected by HIV.

[15] United Nations Children's Fund (UNICEF). 2010. *Children and AIDS: Fifth Stocktaking Report.*

Statement for the Record –
Hearing on The Growing Crisis of Africa's Orphans
Subcommittee on Africa, Global Health, Global Human Rights, and International
Organizations
House Subcommittee on Foreign Affairs
Submitted by Lisa Bos, Senior Policy Advisor for Health, Education and WASH
on behalf of World Vision US

As a Christian relief and development organization committed to serving the needs of children, World Vision has taken particular care to address the needs of orphans and vulnerable children (OVC). Children in Africa, particularly the millions orphaned by the HIV/AIDS epidemic, are susceptible to abuse, child labor, trafficking, dropping out of school and other dangers in addition to other health, psychosocial, economic and social challenges. World Vision works through our own programs and with partners and governments to address critical needs of orphans and provide them with comprehensive, holistic support.

One of the key populations that World Vision works with are children impacted by the AIDS crisis. As reported by UNAIDS, "Despite the modest decline in HIV adult prevalence worldwide and increasing access to treatment, the total number of children aged 0–17 years who have lost their parents due to HIV has not yet declined. Indeed, it has further increased from 14.6 million in 2005 to 16.6 million in 2009."[1] UNICEF estimates for 2013 reflect an increase to 17.8 million children orphaned by AIDS.[2] These estimates do not even include the number of children affected by HIV whose parents are ill and unable to provide adequate care. In addition, current coverage of support for vulnerable children remains extremely low: only 11 percent of highly vulnerable children[3] and their households access essential life-saving and resiliency support services.[4] Research continues to show the differential impact of HIV on children; for example, children affected by AIDS have increased risk of mental health problems, exposure to physical, emotional and sexual abuse, school drop-out,[5] stunting[6] and death.[7]

While the vast majority of OVC can be found living in family situations with an adult caregiver, some of these children live in institutions, in youth-headed households, or on the streets. The epidemic has decimated populations of teachers, healthcare workers, police, and other service providers that help to create strong networks of support for children and adolescents and has

---

[1] Joint United Nations Programme on HIV/AIDS (UNAIDS). 2010. *Global report: UNAIDS report on the global AIDS epidemic 2010.* p. 112.

[2] United Nations Children's Fund (UNICEF). 2013. *Towards an AIDS-Free Generation – Children and AIDS: Sixth Stocktaking Report.*

[3] Current coverage data is drawn from programming that serves children infected or affected by HIV.

[4] United Nations Children's Fund (UNICEF). 2010. *Children and AIDS: Fifth Stocktaking Report.*

[5] Cluver, L. 2011. *Children of the AIDS pandemic.* Nature, 474:27-29.

[6] Ndirangu, M. et al. 2011. *Nutritional status of under-five children in HIV-affected households in western Kenya.* Food and Nutrition Bulletin, 32(2):159-67.

[7] Newell, M.L. et al. 2004. *Mortality of infected and uninfected infants born to HIV-infected mothers in Africa: a pooled analysis.* The Lancet, 364, 9441, 2004:1236-1243.

overburdened the capacity and resources of social service systems. With reduced family and community support, in addition to overwhelmed child welfare systems, OVC are made more vulnerable to abuse and exploitation, and are also more likely to engage in unsafe behaviors, increasing the risk of HIV infection.

As part of the reauthorization of PEPFAR in 2013, Congress maintained the requirement to direct 10% of PEPFAR program funds be directed to OVC activities. This 10% earmark acknowledges the importance of PEPFAR's role in mitigating the impact of HIV/AIDS for the millions of children and adolescents living in affected communities. As PEPFAR's own OVC guidance states, the earmark is intended to not only help children survive, but to help them thrive by "...responding to the social (including economic) and emotional consequences of the disease on children, their families, and communities that support them." [8]

This funding supports child-centered programming targeting the full range of OVC needs at different developmental stages. It is linked with broader development efforts around education, food and nutrition, and livelihood assistance. Community-based OVC programs, like those operated by World Vision, bridge the gaps between medical, social service, and civil society stakeholders, and coordinate support services with prevention, treatment and care programs.

World Vision is currently operating an OVC program, Sustainability Through Economic Strengthening, Prevention and Support for Orphans and Vulnerable Children, Youth and other vulnerable populations (STEPS OVC), in Zambia. This program works with children like eleven-year-old orphan Cleopatra ("Cleo") Mwansa. Cleo lives with her grandmother in Chitulika Village, Mpika. In 2003, Cleo was diagnosed with TB and HIV and was later enrolled by caregivers under St. Joseph's Parish of Mpika Diocese. With STEPS OVC support, caregivers continue to visit Cleo, providing adherence support for her HIV medications, while the Diocese utilizes funding from its Solidarity Fund to pay for Cleo's primary school education.

This story is just one of many showing the importance of OVC programs and the bridge they provide to improving the lives of orphans and vulnerable children. Both Congress' commitment to the 10 percent OVC set-aside and the critical services this funding provides are well documented, which is why it is disconcerting to hear that PEPFAR has taken it upon itself to add pediatric treatment budget codes under the 10 percent earmark. This means rather than focusing this limited funding on a harmonized, multisectoral response to the impact of HIV/AIDS on millions of children and orphans that compliments the already robust clinical treatment portfolio, that a medical response now must be part of the programming. Given that PEPFAR has a strong allocation dedicated to treatment of at least 50 percent of PEPFAR funding, to divert vital funding for OVCs to medical purposes would both disrupt existing programming and distract from the core mission of the OVC set-aside.

---

[8] The U.S. President's Emergency Plan for AIDS Relief. 2012. *Guidance for Orphans and Vulnerable Children Programming*

In addition, if pediatric HIV funding is taken from the OVC earmark it will not only take away funds from OVC programming, but also decrease the overall amount available for pediatric treatment. Our understanding is that the changes being made by the Office of the Global AIDS Coordinator mean that pediatric treatment will no longer be a part of the large treatment set-aside and the budget codes will solely be included under the OVC set-aside. This is a lose-lose for all children affected by HIV. We hope that Congress will take action to restore the 10% OVC set-aside to its original purpose, ensuring funding for children is protected and that improving pediatric treatment gets the attention it deserves through the robust treatment set-aside.

World Vision would also like to highlight the growing orphan crisis in South Sudan. According to the United Nations, more than 380,000 children have been forced from their homes. More than 3,300 of children have been registered as orphaned or separated from their parents since the conflict in South Sudan broke out in December 2013, according to UNICEF, though we believe the actual number may be far higher due to challenges in counting those who are displaced in insecure and remote areas. We hope that the international community will provide more funding needed for family tracing and reunification, including across borders in neighboring countries, as well as scale up funding for interim care arrangements for children who have lost or been separated from their parents.

Finally, World Vision believes that Congressional and Administration action around orphans should be guided by the Action Plan for Children in Adversity. Launched in 2012, the Action Plan unites and aligns 30 offices in seven U.S. Government agencies around the same measurable, achievable goals for international programs relating to vulnerable children. The three main objectives are strong beginnings (ensuring children meet early childhood development milestones), family care first (making sure every child is in a safe family environment), and stronger prevention and response to violence, abuse, neglect, and exploitation. The Action Plan enables U.S. Government agencies to coordinate their efforts to make U.S. programs more effective and efficient in keeping kids alive and allowing them to thrive. World Vision hopes that any legislation that addresses orphans and vulnerable children be in line with the Action Plan and address all three objectives.

Statement for House Foreign Affairs
Sub-Committee on Africa, Global Health, Global Human Rights, and International Organizations

Hearing: The Growing Crisis of Africa's Orphans

Jedd Medefind, President, Christian Alliance for Orphans

Esteemed Chair and Members,

It is no small thing that you have turned the public spotlight of your attention to the orphaned children of Africa. Thank you.

The crisis of Africa's orphans can feel very far off to Americans. We may feel it is "unfortunate," but given the vast hurt of our world, the plight of distant children can appear to be yet one more issue we must regrettably overlook.

I would propose that both America's global interests and her deep tradition of compassionate leadership require otherwise.

Recent projections estimate that more than 10 million children in sub-Saharan Africa have lost both parents.[1] More than five times that number have lost at least one parent. Countless other children live outside of parental care – on the streets, in poorly run orphanages, and/or as victims of a host of exploitative situations.

A fascinating reality about orphans is noted in Malcolm Gladwell's book David and Goliath (more here.) Orphans are statistically much more likely than the average person to grow up to be sociopaths. They are also much more likely than the average person to become world-changing artists, scientists and political leaders.

The watershed line between these contrasting outcomes can be a thin one – often hinging on the actions of a few caring persons, or even just one.

Perhaps it is not too large a logical leap to say that – with its massive population of orphans – Africa itself hinges between two such divergent futures as well.

Along one road we see a continent that is internally tumultuous and externally threatening. Along the other we see a place that still faces its share of challenges, but grows increasingly stable and prosperous, both benefitting and being benefited by the global economy.

The future of Africa's orphans certainly is not the only factor in what will determine which future Africa will own. But the sheer number of orphans in Africa ensures they will have no small impact on this question.

To address the needs of orphans, we must first grasp the severity of their plight. The simple truth is this: *children who face the world without parents are the most vulnerable beings on our planet.*

This vulnerability touches virtually every aspect of an orphan's life. Both single and double orphans are much more likely than other children to be malnourished and stunted in growth.[ii] Even when living with a surviving parent or relatives, orphans are less likely to attend school and more likely to fall behind and drop out.[iii] Orphans often lack funds for basic medical treatment, food, and school supplies.

Orphans are highly prone to labor exploitation. A 2002 assessment in Ethiopia found that more than three quarters of child domestic workers were orphans. Eighty percent of the child domestics interviewed did not have the right to quit their job. They worked over 11 hours per day, with no days off. Most were not allowed to play with their employers' children, listen to the radio or watch TV. More than a third were provided no schooling at all.[iv]

Orphans make ideal victims for sexual exploitation as well. A 2002 assessment in Zambia found that of all children engaged in prostitution, almost half were double orphans and another quarter were single orphans. Their average age was 15 years. Typical daily earnings varied from 63 cents to 7 dollars. These children had sex with three to four clients on an average day.[v]

Of course, the existence of orphans is not new. Myriad ancient documents refer to orphans and also to the obligation within many faith traditions to care for these children.

But in most historical eras, it was relatively uncommon for both parents to die and their children survive. In such cases, extended family could readily absorb an orphaned child. But several factors, especially the advent of global AIDS, have tattered this traditional safety net.

As a widow in Kenya observed, "In the past, people used to care for the orphans and loved them, but these days they are so many, and many people have died who could have assisted them, and therefore orphanhood is a common phenomenon, not strange."[vi]

As anyone who has spent time in African can attest, in many communities a large portion of people of working age have been wiped out. In these places, one often sees a modest number of ailing grandparents struggling to care for a generation of children.

We must have no illusions that help from the United States alone can solve this crisis. In fact, I believe that the only lasting solution ultimately lies *within* Africa.

The US can, however, help encourage and amplify African solutions. We cannot engineer a future in which every orphan knows protection, nurture and belonging. But we can honor, incentivize and support African leadership that works effectively toward that goal.

Three categories of U.S. government action, in particular, can especially help with this.

Supporting Structures that Undergird Economic Growth

First, we must recognize that financial poverty plays a major role in the orphan crisis. The causes of orphanhood are diverse and often tangled, from civil war to disease to substance abuse. But often, financial destitution plays a decisive role. Wherever poverty is dire, all other factors that cause orphanhood are multiplied.

Of course, the power of governments – especially a foreign government – to engineer economic opportunity and growth is tremendously limited. However, the U.S. government can use both soft and hard power to promote and incentivize the political structures that undergird economic growth, from protection of private property and just labor laws to fair courts and transparent government.

Meanwhile, the U.S. can also hold to account the unholy alliances between multi-national corporations and African leaders that extract natural resources from Africa in ways that accrue no benefit to local populations.

Finally, the U.S. government can work in concert with businesses that seek both profit and real growth in the local African economy – through efforts like the Millennium Challenge Corporation. As we have seen powerfully in Asia over recent decades, effective markets within Africa and fair trade beyond it carry potential to lift far more people from poverty than any other means.

Even modest increases in the economic well-being of African families could have a major impact upon the orphan crisis. Improved finances would help preserve struggling families—thus preventing children from becoming orphans—and also provide other families more capacity to take in orphaned children.

Wisely Focused Foreign Aid

The story of foreign aid in Africa – both governmental and private – is highly alloyed at best. I recall hearing Ellen Johnson-Sirleaf, then-President of Liberia, bemoan how billions and billions of dollars in aid have been spent on her continent "with shockingly little result."

And yet, we can identify some areas where the impact of foreign aid has been much more positive than others. Speaking in general terms, we see that government aid can work well when what is most needed is not a highly unique, flexible, personalized product…but rather a commodity that can be mass produced and mass delivered.

Unlike many aspects of human need, the battle against disease often fits this description. Vaccinations, medications and other treatments can be mass produced and mass delivered effectively. And when governments and NGOs do this, it can provide a mass impact for good, from the near eradication of polio to the dramatic reductions in deaths from malaria in areas of targeted effort.

We've seen this with special power via PEPFAR. I've seen firsthand what some call the "Lazarus effect." Skeletal individuals, their bodies riddled with HIV, are brought back to health by consistent ARV treatment. When it is a father or mother that is "resurrected," their children are also saved from becoming orphans. When it is an uncle or aunt or big-hearted neighbor, orphans often receive back their caregivers and providers.

Families

Both common sense and social science affirm a simple truth: children need families.

Children who grow up in orphanages — even relatively well-funded ones – lag behind their peers in virtually every measure, from physical health to intellect to emotional well being, not only as children, but throughout life.

This is not to say that high quality residential care does not provide a vital alternative to life on the streets or in abusive homes. In many parts of the world, the sudden loss of orphanages would mean tragedy for countless children. And even in the long term, the structured and therapeutic environment of quality residential care facilities may be the best feasible option for some children, such as those who have lived for long periods on the streets or have disabilities requiring professional care.

We can honor the many selfless individuals serving children within orphanages and do all we can to help them elevate the quality of care they provide.

But affirming this reality need not obscure the ideal: that every child grow up within a permanent, loving family. This sets before us three clear priorities.

First, preservation of families at risk of disintegration.

Second, reunification of families whenever safely possible.

And third, the creation of new families through adoption – locally if possible, and across regional or international borders when local families cannot be found.

As already alluded to, these are goals government can never achieve on its own. We must be clear about that from the start, or we risk wasteful or even counterproductive efforts.

Governments and large NGOs can indeed marshal and deliver commodities on a vast scale – from food to medicine to shelter. And these commodities are truly vital. But to truly thrive, children require more. They need the love, belonging and nurture that families uniquely provide. And this is not something government alone can provide, no matter how great its resources. It can only be found one caring home at a time.

So to provide for this greatest of all needs – a loving family – even the best government efforts are not direct solutions but indirect. Government cannot "create" loving families, but rather must help support the preservation, reunification and expansion of families.

The U.S. Action Plan on Children in Adversity represents a positive step in this direction. By naming "Family Care" as one of its three foundational objectives, it helped point our global investments decisively in this direction.

The new Children in Families First (CHIFF) legislation currently being considered by Congress also represents a decisively positive development for orphaned children. It would provide a focal point of strong, clear leadership in the U.S. government for the priority of family for children who lack them.

With help from the Action Plan and CHIFF, we have strong reason to hope that the policies and programs of the U.S. government will increasingly champion the needs of the orphans of Africa…and of every other continent as well.

In some cases, this may include financial investment in the work of effective non-profit and civic organizations, both international and local. Even more important, it will include effective non-financial collaboration with these groups.

One essential expression of these collaborative efforts is what we might call a "Permanency Center." Various expressions of this approach are currently being tried, to much good effect, from Costa Rica to South Africa, Rwanda and Uganda to China. Although each local model varies, the central goal is to place children in caring families – permanently whenever possible.

The "Permanency Center" (or whatever the central office is called) serves as the central hub for these efforts. It works to identify the most feasible route to permanency for each child. And then it coordinates among the many actors – from government to local civic groups to international NGOs – in working toward the identified goal. These efforts can range from an NGO's microfinance program that helps struggling families stay together…to a local church's support of reunification efforts…to placement of a child in the home of a welcoming relative….to adoption into a local or international family.

By promoting and supporting innovative models like these, the U.S. government can work closely with African governments to help children experience the one thing they need more than any other: a family.

Conclusion

The need is indeed vast. And the solutions, even for a single child, are so often deeply complex and tangled.

Thankfully, we are anything but alone in this work.

Within African governments – even very imperfect ones – labor many who care deeply about the plight of orphans. Alongside them are countless long-serving organizations, both local and international. In every African community, too, are advocates and champions and quiet servants and caregivers.

Just last month, I attended the first-ever Southern Africa Orphan Summit in South Africa. Some two hundred African pastors and other leaders from across the continent were gathered to engage the question, "How can we as Africans become the primary answer for the needs of Africa's orphans?" As one attendee summed up the spirit of the gathering, "We appreciate Americans and Europeans coming to help us, but these are *our* children and God has called us to their care."

It is my hope that Africa's future belongs to bold and sacrificial individuals such as these!

The story of Africa's orphans today hangs in the balance between bright hope and continued turmoil. In many ways, this story mirrors that of the continent as well.

Chapter one is in large part tragic. But what makes a book a tragedy is not its start, but its finish. And we have strong reason to hope that together – governments and nonprofits, civic and faith-based groups, foreigners who love Africa and especially Africans themselves – we will write a future that is rich in hope for the orphans of Africa...and for all of the continent besides.

---

[i] http://www.unaids.org/en/media/unaids/contentassets/documents/unaidspublication/2013/20131129_stocktaking_report_children_aids_en.pdf

[ii] See, for example, Ainsworth, M. and J. Semali, *The Impact of Adult Deaths on Children's Health in Northwestern Tanzania*, Policy Research Working Paper No. 2266, (Washington, D. C.: World Band, 2000). Or Lindblade, K. A., et al., "Health and nutritional status of orphans <6 years old cared for by relatives in western Kenya," *Tropical Medicine and International Health*, vol. 8, no. 1, 2003, pp. 67-72. Or the *National Nutrition and EPI Survey*, Ministry of Health and Child Welfare, Harare, Zimbabwe, 2003.

[iii] See, for example, Case, A., C. Paxson, and J. Ableidinger, *Orphans in Africa*. (New Jersey: Princeton University Center for Health and Wellbeing, Research Program in Development Studies, January 2003). Or Hyde, K., et al., "HIV/AIDS and Education in Uganda: Window of opportunity?", Paper supported by the Rockefeller Foundation, January 2002.

[iv] Kifle, A., *Ethiopia – Child Domestic Workers in Addis Ababa: A Rapid Assessment*, (Geneva: International Labour Organization, International Programme on the Elimination of Child Labour, July 2002).

[v] Mushingeh, A., et al., *HIV/AIDS and Child Labour in Zambia: A rapid assessment on the case of the Lusaka, Copperbelt and Eastern Provinces*, Paper No. 5, (Geneva/Lusaka: International Labour Organization, International Programme on the Elimination of Child Labour, August 2002).

[vi] Widow's quote from UNICEF publication, "Africa's Orphaned Generations," originally appeared in Nyambedha, Erick Otieno, Simiyu Wandibba and Jens Aagaard-Hansen, 'Changing patterns of orphan care due to the HIV epidemic in western Kenya', Social Science & Medicine, vol. 57, no. 2, July 2003, pp. 301-311.